DÜRER

LIFT PICTURE FOR TITLE AND COMMENTARY

ALBRECHT
DÜRER

TEXT BY

H. T. MUSPER

THE LIBRARY OF GREAT PAINTERS

THAMES AND HUDSON · LONDON

Translated by Robert Erich Wolf

First published in Great Britain in 1966

CONTENTS

COLOUR PLATES

1. Hans Schwarz: MEDAL WITH PORTRAIT OF DÜRER.
Boxwood. *Herzog Anton Ulrich Museum, Braunschweig*

Dürer's family came from Hungary, but they seem to have been Germans who emigrated and then returned to their homeland. Their Christian names without exception were all German. True, one of their cousins in Cologne called himself Unger rather than Dürer, but his first name remained Lasslen and not Ladislaus or Laszlo as it would have been in Hungarian. The place from which the Dürers came was the village of Ajtós which no longer exists but was near the city of Gyula, thirty-odd miles north of Arad. In Hungarian *Ajtó* means "door," *Türe* in German, whence Dürer. The coat of arms Dürer designed for himself in 1523 contained a wide-open door, and this speaks for itself.

The artist's father, Albrecht Dürer the Elder, was a goldsmith in Nuremberg and as such was highly regarded. We know what he looked like from a drawing by his fifteen-year-old son (W 3), the portrait in Florence, and the even more expressive one at seventy in London. In the family chronicle and the fragment of his memoirs which has come down to us, the son wrote out a touching account of the life and death of his father.

Barbara the mother, born Holper, lived to be sixty-two. Dürer must have felt very close to her. After the death of his father in 1502, he took her to live in his own household, and in his letters from Venice he inquired after her more often than after his wife. The portrait in charcoal made in 1514, the year she died, belongs among the highest achievements of German art (W 559, fig. 28). Her last hours are recorded in her son's diary, a precious document of the life and trials of a devout woman who bore eighteen children, withstood plague, illness, and privation with unflagging patience though people railed against her, and fought to the last against death although she never feared "to stand before God."

Albrecht Dürer the Younger, the painter, was born in Nuremberg on May 21, 1471, the third child and second son. Of his early development the family chronicle tells us: "And my father took special plea-

2. THE DÜRER HOUSE AT THE TIERGÄRTNER GATE IN NUREMBERG

sure in me. For he saw that I was eager to know how to do things and I learned to read and write [he first attended the Latin school of the church of St. Lawrence], and so he taught me the goldsmith's trade, and though I could do that work as neatly as you could wish, my heart was more for painting than for that kind of work. I raised the whole question with my father, and he was far from happy about it, regretting all the time wasted, but just the same he gave in and apprenticed me [1486–89] to Michael Wolgemut. In those years God gave me the will to learn, but I had to put up with much annoyance from my master's other lads."

About the years which followed we know less from Dürer himself than from *Christophorus Scheurls Lobrede auf Anton Kress* (a panegyric printed in Willibald Pirckheimer's *Opera*, Frankfurt, 1610), namely that he traveled all over Germany (*peragrata Germania*), and since the Netherlands were part of the Holy Roman Empire, it is likely that he went there also. In 1492 he reached Colmar on the Upper Rhine where he became acquainted with the brother of the great engraver Martin Schongauer, who had died four years before. It is certain that he worked for various printers in

Basel and Strassburg. In the latter town he painted the lost portraits of his master and his master's wife, and at Darmstadt he had at least a hand in a large share of the St. Dominic altarpiece of which only fragments survive (page 59).

Upon his return to Nuremberg, he did not become a Master in a guild since, as Thausing showed, painting in that city was esteemed as a "free" or "liberal" art and not considered among the crafts. When he set up his own workshop with his own apprentices, and what may have led him to do so, is not known, but it certainly must not have been before his return in 1495 from his first journey to Italy.

As was the custom of the times, it was his father who arranged his marriage on May 18, 1494, to Agnes Frey, the daughter of a much-esteemed master in fine metalwork.

Two years after Dürer's death, Willibald Pirckheimer had much to say about Agnes in a letter to the master builder Johann Tscherte, and none of it was flattering. He described her as nagging, jealous, and shrewish, accused her of old-fogyish piety, petty stinginess, and greed, and even went so far as to blame her for making Dürer's life a hell on earth and hastening his all too early death. In her favor speaks the fact that, married to her, Dürer accomplished a life work, the work of a genius, which demanded incomparably great effort and concentration and solid nerves, and this no man is likely to achieve if plagued by such a wife as Pirckheimer described. What is more, Dürer portrayed her over and over again, in her youth and old age, and took her with him on his journey to the Netherlands. Before judging her harshly, we should remember that in those times the role of a wife was quite different, and this is shown in many small ways: Dürer begged a gratuity for his wife from a gentleman who was commissioning a picture; in the Netherlands, when her husband received persons of importance, Agnes ate in the kitchen along with the maid; the task fell to her, as to his mother, of hawking woodcuts and engravings by her husband and other artists in the open market place in Nuremberg at Christmas and in Augsburg, Frankfurt, and Ingolstadt during the great fairs.

And yet, in the fall of the very year of his marriage, Dürer left his young bride to go off on his first trip to Italy. But that may not have had anything to do with his feelings toward her. More likely the decision to go at that time was taken or hastened because there was an epidemic of plague in Nuremberg. From a moral point of view, to quit one's city and leave one's wife behind to face the perils alone had nothing infamous about it. Even the physician Hieronymus Münzer did likewise, claiming that *illum minime in bello et peste mori, qui in eis non esset*—"the man least likely to perish by war or plague is the one who is elsewhere." The twenty-three-year-old artist chose to reach Venice by the route over the Brenner Pass via Trent. He probably went on horseback along with other travelers, as a letter to Pirckheimer from Venice suggests. The regular post connection between Innsbruck and Milan organized by Franz von Taxis (as the Postal Museum in Bern kindly informs me) was just beginning at that time and involved only messengers on horseback. There were as yet no roads carriages could take for long distances. Dürer's impressions on the way and in Venice were of momentous significance. He was no modern traveler out only to sip the delights of the city on the lagoon. Rather, he was set on making his own what the Italian painters had achieved, and this meant, above all, mastery of the nude and of the means of depicting space. Toward this end he made copies from Mantegna, Credi, Pollaiuolo, and others. Today we can scarcely imagine what excitement must have possessed the young artist as he strode across the Piazza. It is very possible that he saw his friend Pirckheimer, who had been studying for some years in Padua and Pavia where he had come to understand the teachings of the Italian Neoplatonists.

By early 1495 Dürer had returned to Nuremberg and entered into relations with the Elector Frederick the Wise of Saxony, from whom he had already received various commissions. He set to engraving in earnest and made a beginning on the great work of his youth, the large-format woodcut series of the Apocalypse, which he finally published in 1498. This was for him a time of unquenchable productivity in both painting and graphic work, and in painting at least he reached a peak in his self-portrait of 1500 (page 83).

When the apocalyptic destruction of the world everyone expected in that year did not take place, there was a universal sigh of relief. With 1500, then, began the period when a new Dürer blossomed, joyful, open to the good things of life. The woodcut series of the Life of Mary belongs to this new mood, and the mass of studies in proportion he turned out in the first years of the new century culminated in the engraved *Adam and Eve* of 1504 (fig. 12).

Whether it was that a new wave of plague provided the excuse or because the Augsburg humanist Peutinger let him know that there might be an important

3. LOVERS. 1492–93. Pen drawing. *Kunsthalle, Hamburg*

commission from the German merchants in Venice, once again, in the late summer of 1505, Dürer headed south. This time he remained in Venice for more than a year, until January 1507, not without occasional excursions out of the city, to Padua for instance (where his portrait appears in a fresco attributed to Domenico Campagnola) and to Bologna—"for the sake of art, to learn the secrets of perspective." Trips to Florence and Rome cannot be ruled out: "When the Emperor comes to Italy [for his coronation]," he wrote, "I should like to accompany him to Rome." After his signature on a copy of his painting *Christ among the Doctors* of 1506 appears the word "Romae."

For almost half a year Dürer worked on *The Madonna of the Rose Garlands* (fig. 16), the painting commissioned by the German merchants for San Bartolommeo, the church of their corporation from which those of them who died abroad were buried. Ten letters to his friend Willibald Pirckheimer written in what must have been a jocund and relaxed mood afford a unique glimpse into the world in which he lived in Venice with artists and merchants as companions. From them

4. SELF-PORTRAIT. C. 1491. Pen drawing. *University Library, Erlangen*

we learn also how highly esteemed he was: the city of Venice offered him two hundred ducats to remain in its service for a year. Small wonder that he ended the last letter exclaiming: "Here I am a gentleman, at home a toady!" He praises the Venetians as "noble souls, civil companions" who on the one hand are "models of virtue but at the same time are the most two-faced lying thievish scoundrels in the world." He took a dim view of Pirckheimer's request that he purchase for him rings, pearls, sapphires, rubies, emeralds, diamonds, glasswork, and carpets with which his friend hoped to set up business in Nuremberg, but carried out his wishes because he had borrowed money from Pirckheimer and felt himself obligated to return the kindness. That Dürer himself delighted in such things became more and more obvious. Everyone wished him well, he wrote, right up to the chief citizens. Only a few of his colleagues were envious, but even they were forced to admire him, admitting that "they had never seen more sublime, more enchanting paintings and

5. LOBSTER. 1495. Pen drawing. *State Museums, Berlin-Dahlem*

more beautiful colors." Giovanni Bellini, whom Dürer judged to be "the best in painting," praised him highly in the presence of the most prominent dignitaries. But everything was not pure bliss. There were gloomier moods and less happy occurrences, and there was talk of courtesans and whores and the dread of "the French sickness" (syphilis, epidemic at the time).

Home again, he painted the *Adam and Eve* (page 105) and, under commission from Frederick the Wise, *The Martyrdom of the Ten Thousand* (in Vienna). From mid-1508 to 1509 he worked on the principal panel for the altarpiece of the Heller chapel, *The Assumption and Coronation of the Virgin*, on whose wings not only his brother Hans helped but also no less an artist than Matthias Grünewald, who executed four grisailles. Nine letters exchanged with his patron, the merchant Jakob Heller in Frankfurt, tell us much about the way in which Dürer worked at his painting. The preparation of the wooden panel was entrusted to an assistant, who also coated it with gold where required. The artist himself then saw to the underpainting, first laying down four to six coats of the most expensive color, ultramarine (prepared from lapis lazuli). He then underpainted the whole several times more. When it was sufficiently dry, he began the final

underdrawing, probably in watercolor. In spite of their many coats of underpainting, Dürer's paintings impress one as extraordinarily thin, as Doerner pointed out. All this was done so that his pictures might last for centuries, and so it is so much the more tragic that the central panel of the Heller altarpiece was destroyed in the fire which ravaged the Munich Residence Palace in 1729: all that survives to tell us of its beauty are the very fine preliminary drawings.

We have a pretty good idea of why Dürer dunned the merchant Jakob Heller for more and more money over and above the original price of the altarpiece: in 1509 he acquired the splendid house he had been living in for some time at the Tiergärtner Gate at the lower end of the Burg, the house visitors today know as the Dürer House (fig. 2).

After Anton Koberger had placed a printing press at his disposal, Dürer brought out in book form in 1511 the Great and the Small Woodcut Passions, the Life of Mary, and the Apocalypse. These were followed in 1513 by the Engraved Passion, and there were also a great many single woodcuts and copperplate engravings.

Dürer was now named an honorary citizen of the Great Council of his native city. He was linked in

7. MADONNA AND CHILD. *Dealer's collection*

ILLVSTRISSIMÆ. ET EXCELLENTISSIMÆ. DÑÊ. DOMINÆ. ALATHEÆ. TAL-
bot, Arundeliæ, & Surriæ, Comitissæ, etc: hanc tabellam olim ab Alberto Durero ad uiuum depic-
tam, iamq̃ in Collectione Arundeliana conseruatam, & a Wenceslao Hollar Bohemo Aqua forti æri
insculptam, humillimè offert et dedicat.   Adam Alexius Bierling   Antuerpiæ Anno. 1646.

6. YOUNG WOMAN OF THE FÜRLEGER FAMILY.
Engraving by Wenzel Hollar after a lost portrait by Dürer

friendship with the Imperial astronomers Stabius and Heinfogel for whom he drew two charts of the heavens. From 1512 on, his connection with Emperor Maximilian I proved highly fruitful, with fine commissions for the margin designs for the prayer book, specially printed on parchment, prepared for the Emperor in Augsburg, as well as for the *Triumphal Arch* and the *Triumphal Procession*. In 1515 the Emperor awarded him a life annuity of a hundred guilders a year to be paid from the Nuremberg city treasury and toward which the Emperor paid his share. That was also the year in which he exchanged drawings with Raphael (two nudes now in the Albertina). In the course of the Augsburg Parliament of 1518, where he met many famous men and drew portraits of Hans Burgkmair, Count Solms, and Jakob Fugger, he set down the first studies for the two painted portraits and the gold-plate woodcut of the Emperor, who, however, died at the beginning of the following year. Among other celebrities with whom he came in contact was the reformer Ulrich Zwingli whose acquaintance he made in Zurich while traveling in Switzerland in 1519.

But soon Dürer had to embark on a longer journey, this time to the Netherlands, and for a special reason. After Maximilian's death, the Emperor's annuity to Dürer had to be re-confirmed by his successor, and the petition had to be presented in person.

Although he had a specific destination for this journey, Dürer availed himself of the chance to travel to many places, to acquaint himself with the country and its people as well as everything it might contain of interest in art and nature. Because he was not only world-famous but also had great personal charm, he won the affection of everyone he met.

On July 12, 1520, in the company of his wife and their maidservant, he set off on this new adventure. The Bishop of Bamberg, to whom he was no stranger, supplied him—in exchange for a painting of the Virgin plus woodcuts and engravings—with a customs permit and three letters of introduction. Without these a journey across the many borders which lay ahead would have been impossible. For Dürer carried with him chests and bales crammed with engravings, not his alone but also those of artists like Hans Baldung Grien and H. L. Schäufelein. Such things were considered no more than run-of-the-mill tradesmen's wares and would have been taxed accordingly were it not for the good Bishop's letters. More than once he was obliged to leave behind a part of his goods as security to be returned to him on the homeward journey. We know all this from the journal Dürer kept up on his travels along with two sketchbooks, one for drawings in ink, the other for silverpoint. The journal has come down to us in fragmentary copies only, but it is of priceless value and not merely because it is one of the very few such documents of the time. In it Dürer noted down in detail even the smallest expenditures and every gift he gave or received. His medium of exchange was his art. He had not entered these unknown territories with empty hands: his very desirable engravings could be bartered for almost anything. Through them he won friends of imposing prestige: the Portuguese agents, in particular Rodrigo d'Almada; the Genoese silk merchants Tommaso and Gherardo Bombelli; representatives of the Nuremberg merchant princes such as Alexander Imhoff who was the deputy of the Fuggers; and the Nuremberg town councilors who were charged with bringing the Imperial treasure to Aachen. But above all it was the most eminent artists in every region he passed through who sought his company. He was invited to countless banquets and social occasions, joined only rarely by his wife and maid, who presumably preferred to remain behind. Dürer himself loved such signs of success and the company of distinguished society where he could shine. He reports that "the painters set out everything in silver plates with all sorts of expensive trimmings and the most costly foods. Their wives all attended on them, and when I was led in to the table the entire company lined up on either side as if some great man were being introduced. Among them were also certain very distinguished personages, all of whom bowed low before me and addressed me with the greatest humility."

In Cologne he left the boat in which he had been

8. ST. EUSTACE. 1500-1502. Engraving

traveling and proceeded overland to Antwerp, where he found a warm welcome and good quarters with the innkeeper Jobst Planckfelt. His stay in Antwerp was frequently interrupted by visits to Malines and Brussels, and once he ventured as far as Zeeland to see a whale but arrived too late: the great beast had been dumped back into the sea. On that occasion he barely escaped with his life. Caught in a storm, he himself had to lend a hand to keep the ship from foundering. In Ghent he studied the great altarpiece by the brothers Van Eyck, and in Bruges pictures by Rogier van der Weyden and by "a great old master" as well as the gleaming white marble Madonna by Michelangelo. At the beginning of October he went off for a two months' stay in Aachen, where he witnessed the fantastic coronation of Charles V and was much taken by the "well-proportioned columns and their fine capitals in porphyry, green, red, and granite" which had been brought to the Cathedral from Ravenna by Charlemagne. Then he went on to Cologne, where in the Emperor's festive hall (later called the Gürzenich) he attended princely balls and lavishly ordered banquets and where he was at last rewarded with the object of his voyage, confirmation of his annuity. Besides all this, he also availed himself of the chance of seeing the great altarpiece of the Three Kings by Stefan Lochner, whose name was for the first time restored to public glory by Dürer's praise.

Old towns and buildings both sacred and secular fascinated him, and he packed his sketchbook with drawings of them. In his journal he expressed himself about art in a way that was not to become the rule for many years yet, pronouncing entirely personal judgments on what he saw and often praising things with the simple word "good." He received invitations from the Antwerp town council and also from the Vice-regent Margaret, whose behavior, however, was perplexing: on the one hand she volunteered to further his cause with the Emperor, but on the other hand made no secret of her dissatisfaction with the portrait of her father, Emperor Maximilian, which he had brought with him.

Dürer's admiration was much excited by the works of his colleagues Massys, Mostaert, Orley, Van Leyden, Patinir (who invited him to his wedding), Provost, Vellert, and Gossaert as well as of the sculptor Conrad Meit of Worms, for whom he had special esteem. Not that he could not be critical, but his reservations were never made out of envy. The most famous among these artists became his friends. They joined often in lively gatherings, and he preserved the features of many of them in drawings. In Malines he saw again Jacopo de' Barbari, whom he did not find particularly sympathetic.

Everything strange and out of the ordinary, anything exotic whether in nature or art, delighted Dürer as something miraculous. In Brussels he could gaze his fill on the gold and silver treasures of Montezuma which Spain had seized from Mexico. Horns and claws of every kind of animal fascinated him, and he sent home a large tortoise shell and an immense fish bone. Parrots filled him with enthusiasm, as did Chinese porcelain vessels, conch shells, bits of coral, ivory artifacts, and also costly velvets, silks, satins, and rare furs. That he was a gourmand we know from his frequent mention of oysters, home-made preserves, sweets,

marzipan, pieces of sugar cane, capers, olives, candied lemon peel, coconuts. A good deal of this he received in the way of gifts from his Portuguese friends; some he may have taken as "medicine." Curiously enough, he sometimes bought things in quantity, as if hoarding for the future: a dozen pairs of ladies' gloves, a half-dozen Netherlandish hoods, and the like. He was quite unperturbed when in church a thief cut off the girdle in which his wife carried her money and keys, and yet he noted down punctiliously that six individuals he had portrayed never gave him so much as a penny for his efforts. "I lost out on all the work, drawings, sales, and other dealings I did in the Netherlands, and most of all Dame Margaret paid me absolutely nothing for everything I gave her and made for her," was the way he summed up the great journey.

For all that, life could have rolled on in customary comfort, but suddenly, soon after Whitsuntide of 1521, rumors spread that Luther had been taken prisoner. To his journal Dürer confided a long lament and a touching prayer. He feared that the holy man who "had delivered me from great anxiety" might be made away with, little suspecting that the imprisonment was a measure arranged with the Elector Frederick the Wise for Luther's own protection. In Luther, Dürer saw above all else the man who would deliver Christendom from what he thought of as the decadent Papacy and who would bring men back to the pure lessons of Christ, but his thoughts turned also to the Jews, Muscovites, Russians, and Greeks who, by fault of the Popes, had become "separated" from the One Church. Were Luther to die, Dürer hoped—naïvely, as we now know—that his mission would be carried on by Erasmus of Rotterdam, whom he had portrayed in the latter part of 1520, the same Erasmus who two years later shut his door to the wounded, bleeding Hutten for fear of becoming compromised.

And so, after almost a year, the journey was somewhat hurriedly broken off. It cannot be ruled out that Dürer may have expressed his opinions too freely and realized too late how precarious was his position. The fact is, in Antwerp he had often frequented the Saxon Augustinians, who had founded a settlement there in 1513. Their prior, Jakob Propst, was one of the most fiery partisans of Luther's ideas, and soon was forced to flee back to Germany, to Nuremberg. His colleague, Prior Heinrich van Zutphen, was likewise expelled and shamefully mistreated by the German Catholics and at last burned at the stake.

In Brussels Dürer portrayed the King of Denmark,

9. THE FOUR HORSEMEN OF THE APOCALYPSE. 1498. Woodcut

10. JOACHIM AND ST. ANNE MEETING AT THE GOLDEN GATE.
From the Life of Mary series. 1504. Woodcut

Just as during his years in Italy, so also on this expedition to the North, Dürer worked hard. According to his journal, he painted not only the *St. Jerome* (page 127), now in Lisbon, but also six portraits in oil, not all of which have survived. In addition, he turned out many important portrait sketches in charcoal as well as some deeply moving ink drawings of the Passion. Especially fine are the silverpoint drawings in the sketchbook.

In Nuremberg, to which he returned in August 1521, not all of his dreams were to be realized. He never had the opportunity to carry out a large *Madonna and Saints* for which he had already drawn several of the heads, nor an engraving of the Crucifixion. The times were too disturbed. Hans Denk, Rector of the Sebaldus School, was stirring up trouble. Friends and pupils of Dürer declared themselves outright atheists and were banished from the city. Anabaptists and fanatics upset the public order, called for doing away with all private property. Finally, in spite of threats from the Bishop of Bamberg and the Emperor and without regard for the ravages of the Peasant Revolt, in 1525 the Nuremberg town council came out officially for the new teachings.

During his last years Dürer devoted himself to intensive work on his theoretical books, which were published in 1525, 1527, and, posthumously, in 1528. This was the time also when he set down the Family Chronicle and the Memoirs, the source of so much valuable information about the man and his work. And yet he did not leave off painting. One after the other, as if nothing could dam up the flow, he turned out portraits, some among them of the highest significance. His working life closed with what he intended as his last testament, *The Four Apostles* (pages 139 and 141).

On April 6, 1528, Dürer died, apparently from malaria caught in previous years on his excursion to the island of Zeeland. He had not reached even his fifty-seventh year.

who, like him, was a petitioner to Charles V, claiming the dowry promised to his wife Isabella, the Emperor's sister. Once king of all Scandinavia, he was driven out of his country and fled to Brussels to beg the Emperor's help after the blood-bath in Stockholm when he attempted to avenge himself on his opponents. The portrait has not come down to us but is known from the preparatory charcoal sketch (W 815). Dürer did not return to Antwerp but went directly to Cologne, and it is there that his journal breaks off.

11. THE PAUMGARTNER ALTARPIECE. 1502–4. *Alte Pinakothek, Munich*

DRAWINGS

Nearly a thousand drawings by Dürer have come down to us. If to these are added the constructions designed to illustrate his theories, the number is even higher, and still many drawings of all kinds must have been lost. One must distinguish between sketches or studies done for the artist's own purposes with no intention of having them seen by others as against those drawings which are fully worked out and as finished as any other picture; for these latter, the designation "master drawings" has been coined.

Dürer employed every kind of technique. In his early years he preferred pen and ink, combined at times with wash or watercolor. After 1500 he took to charcoal or chalk, though it is not always easy to decide in a particular drawing which he used. Right from the outset he mastered the technique of silverpoint on a prepared ground, and in the 1520s he favored a metal point on colored paper for work in large format. Also, the distinction must be made between his graphic

work in the narrowest sense and the painstaking, truly pictorial drawings done with a brush on bluish, green, or brown paper using shading, halftones, and white highlights, a technique he learned in Venice and developed to virtuoso heights. Winkler says, "He drew with the brush the way most artists can draw with only the sharpest pen." The wash drawings and gouaches done with a fine brush date from his first trip to Italy or even earlier. Mostly, the first jottings of his ideas were dashed off with a goose-quill pen or, often, with merely a lead stylus, and yet so great was his skill that even with such limited means he could pin down the most sensitive impressions from nature.

As splendid examples of pen drawings of the earliest period we can single out the *Self-Portrait with Upraised Hand* (fig. 4) and the sheet in New York with studies of hands and cushions which can be dated 1493 (W 27) together with two drawings of the Holy Family (W 25, W 30), the *Nude Woman* of 1493 (W 28), the *Lovers* (fig. 3)—that sketch brimming over with delight in life—and the recently lost *Women's Bathhouse* from

12. ADAM AND EVE. 1504. Engraving

of 1511 (fig. 21) and seven versions of the Holy Family (W 514–20).

The illustrations for Emperor Maximilian's prayer book (fig. 33) date from the middle of the second decade of the sixteenth century. A few groups of nudes from that same time (W 666, 667) sum up the artist's long-standing preoccupation with the human body.

Seemingly intended for a never executed woodcut Passion in oblong format were the highly significant and very expressive drawings of 1520, 1521, and 1524 (W 793–98), which are matched in quality by only a few others, a *Crucifixion*, a *Pietà*, and an *Entombment* (W 880–82). There are very fine sketches dated 1522 for a *Madonna and Saints* which was never carried through, and we still have the studies for the engraved portraits of Frederick the Wise and Melanchthon.

In the early period, Dürer brought out forms by cross-hatching, but around 1500 he abandoned this in favor of parallel hatching in the attempt to model forms with greater definition than his previous technique had permitted.

Dürer used charcoal for the first time in 1503 for certain portraits, among them that of Willibald Pirckheimer (W 270), and for religious subjects including the starkly expressive foreshortened head of *The Man of Sorrows* (W 272), the terrifying *Head of a Suffering Man* (W 271), the extremely foreshortened *Dead Christ* of 1505 (W 378), and its contemporary *Head of John the Baptist* (fig. 13). The *Memento mei* (fig. 15) from the same year would be unthinkable in any other technique. Charcoal was used also for what is perhaps the deepest and most personal statement Dürer ever made, the portrait of his mother of 1514 (fig. 28). There is somewhat more feeling for tonal values in the *Emperor Maximilian I* (W 567) which Dürer drew from life "in the tiny room at the top of the palace in Augsburg." A great many portrait heads, mostly of men, were drawn during the Netherlands trip and toward the end of his life, among them the "*Lerse*" (W 804) and the so-called *Bridegroom* (W 807), the study for the woodcut portrait of Ulrich Varnbüler (W 908), and the half-length figures of bearded men (W 915, 916). The superb portrait from around 1521 of Cardinal Lang von Wellenburg, only recently discovered (fig. 46), and the heads of St. Barbara (W 845) and St. Apollonia (W 846), which were studies for the *Madonna and Saints*, as well as some very beautiful drawings of drapery (W 840–44), all seem to have been done in chalk.

In his earliest years Dürer achieved mastery in the

1496 (W 152). Only a single sheet, *Horsemen in the Harbor* (W 49), gives us some notion of what the undoubtedly numerous but now lost preparatory studies for the Apocalypse and the Large Passion must have looked like. This technique was also used for the costume studies of Venetian women (W 73–76) made in Venice in 1494 while doing copies after Mantegna and other artists, and again soon after 1500 in the sketches for the Green Passion and the Life of Mary as well as for other woodcuts and copper engravings. While landscapes done by pen are rare, from the early period there is a study of rocks (W 57), from the middle period the *Hamlet of Heroldsberg* of 1510 (W 481), from the Netherlands journey that finest product of graphic insight *The Harbor at Antwerp* (fig. 34), and from his last years the *Fortifications with Mountains and Sea* (W 942). Among the very finest ink drawings belong *The Rest on the Flight into Egypt*

13. HEAD OF JOHN THE BAPTIST. Charcoal drawing. *Albertina, Vienna*

silverpoint technique, thereby continuing a tradition which had come down from the Van Eycks. But for many decades after his *Self-Portrait at Thirteen* (W 1), a remarkable foretaste of his genius, and the portrait of his father (W 3), he scarcely ever turned to it, and it was not until he set out for the Netherlands that he remembered this especially adaptable technique, but then he filled an entire sketchbook with silverpoint drawings. Along with these should be mentioned portraits of Lucas van Leyden (W 816), Sebastian Brant (?) (W 817), the Moor Catherine (W 818), a woman (W 907, from 1523), the study for the engraving of Cardinal Albrecht von Brandenburg (W 896), and Lucas Cranach the Elder (W 898, from 1524). Other than these, he used silverpoint only for one Passion study, the *Mourning over the Dead Christ* (W 883), and in the middle period for a single landscape, the *Wire-Drawing Mill* (W 480).

Since silverpoint was adaptable only to smaller formats, for larger drawings on prepared paper Dürer employed a metal point, a pewter stylus. However, it is not always easy to determine if a particular drawing was done in this technique or in charcoal or chalk. He

had recourse to it in his later years for many important drawings, including the portrait of his wife done in Antwerp (W 814), the very fine preliminary studies done between 1521 and 1523 for the never executed Crucifixion engraving (the Women at the Cross, John, Magdalen, the crucified Christ, the weeping angels' heads, W 858–64), the *Temptation of St. Anthony* (W 884) and the *Virgin Reading* (W 885), both from 1521, as well as the head of St. Joseph (W 848) for the *Madonna and Saints*, and finally the extremely significant studies done in 1523 and 1525 for *The Four Apostles* (W 873, 878) and those of 1526 for their heads (fig. 44), to which list can be added a few other figures. In certain drawings (W 866–69) it is difficult to be sure what medium was used, and there is much argument about the portrait of Lord Morley, Henry VIII's chancellor who brought the Order of the Garter to Archduke Ferdinand of Austria (W 912), about those from 1525 presumed to be of the Margravines of Brandenburg-Ansbach (W 913, 914), and about the *Ulrich Starck* of 1527 (W 919).

Brush drawings with wash by Dürer are known from as far back as the Venice period when he did,

14. THE GREAT HORSE. 1505. Engraving

among others, the *Female Nude* of 1495 (W 85), the charming *Madonna in a Niche* (W 142), the *Shrimp* (W 92), which is a very fine bright-toned watercolor in pungent rose, and apparently the large and dashing *Flag Lily* in the Escorial (W 348). The outstanding examples from the following period include the colored *Horseman* of 1498 (W 176) and the *Jousting Helmet Viewed from Three Sides* (W 177).

Beginning with his second stay in Italy, Dürer took to making brush studies of details whenever he was preparing paintings involving several figures. Such drawings acquire special importance when the final painting was later lost, as happened with the Heller altarpiece, or when the project was apparently never carried through, as in the case of the *Madonna and Saints*. Heightening with white was introduced when the artist utilized papers with a colored ground, first of all for the Green Passion series of 1504. The studies for *The Madonna of the Rose Garlands* of 1506 were done on a very choice Venetian blue-tinted paper, as were the *Female Nude Seen from the Rear* (fig. 18) and the *Woman's Head* (W 403). Those for the Heller altarpiece

of 1508, for the most part on paper with a green ground, no longer have that painterly transparent quality the Venetian atmosphere had stimulated him to, but nevertheless avoid any recourse to pen drawing. They are stronger and tend more to emphasize textural values, like the figures and heads of Apostles, among which there is one head Robert Vischer described as "absurd, superclever, hospitalsick" (fig. 17), and also various studies of hands joined in prayer, soles of feet, and draperies.

During his time in the Netherlands, Dürer returned to this medium for the portrait of the Portuguese agent Rodrigo d'Almada (W 813) and the extraordinary studies for the Lisbon *St. Jerome*, which include the drawing of a ninety-three-year-old man done in Antwerp (W 788–92). A brilliant study of drapery (W 835) likewise is dated 1521.

Among the drawings a special place must be reserved for the landscape sketches, most of them done in the southern Tyrol in the course of the first trip to Italy. For these he used watercolor or gouache plus pen on white paper. Most of them were left as mere sketches, but some were painstakingly completed, in part with touches added with a fine metal point. They are the first such pictures to aim at setting down a view of some particular locality, and it is especially sad that more than a half-dozen of them, once in Bremen, were lost during the last war.

The *Wire-Drawing Mill* (W 61) and the lost *St. John's Cemetery* (W 62), with their surfaces which are still quite flat and without any lines suggesting depth, are so "primitive" as to make it likely that they date from 1489 when the artist was still influenced by the Wolgemut workshop.

In the fall of 1494 Dürer set out for Italy by way of Innsbruck, of which he did an overall view (W 66) and two glimpses of the Castle (W 67, 68). From there his route led through Trent, and on the way he did the lost *View of Klausen*, which a few years later served for the background of the *Nemesis* engraving (B 77). In Trent itself he painted the wonderfully colored *View of the City* (W 96) and the *View of the Castle* (W 95) and the nearby mountain, the *Trintberg* (W 97). A detour via Lake Garda provided the occasion for the *Arco* (page 65), in which the subtle technique is pushed to its farthest point.

Most of these are a superb mixture of broadly laid down tonal or color washes in which brushwork as precise and fine as in miniature painting was used specifically for cliffs, rocks, and trees and for hair-thin pen outlines of houses, castles, villages, and the like. This can be seen in *Pass in the Alps* (W 100), *Ruin on a Rock with Water* (W 98), and *Italian Mountain* (in Dürer's uniquely expressive German, *Wehlsch pirg*) (page 63). Some are no more than quick sketches: *Hut in the Mountains* (W 102), *Cluster of Trees in a Mountainous Landscape* (W 104), and *Cliff Face with Withered Shrubbery* (W 111), which much later was used for the background in the engraving of *Knight, Death, and Devil* (fig. 27). A few sketches of isolated trees (W 112, 121) also date from this journey.

There is almost no way we can know now whether Dürer kept a sketchbook with him always or set up individual sheets, and how he carried about the necessary equipment. As to the question whether the watercolors were done en route to Italy or on the homeward journey, the present writer has presented his arguments elsewhere. Suffice it to say here that it goes against the grain to imagine that they were not dashed off in the excitement of first discovery. They bear too many marks of an innocent spontaneity, which could scarcely have been Dürer's after his experiences in Venice. With what he learned there, he could not have had such a peculiarly personal vision but would have thought of his landscapes in terms borrowed from Bellini, Cima, or Carpaccio. True, there are specialists in the matter who argue that the trees Dürer paints are still in leaf, but it can be answered that this is entirely possible in October. In any event, it is quite mistaken to think of Dürer as a kind of Impressionist whose only aim was to capture fleeting external optical appearances. The fact is that those, when they occur, are exceptions in his work. Much more fascinating to him than naturalistic effects was what he could create with no more than a box of watercolors. Indeed, there was in him something we can call conscious formalism or even mannerism. He was, for example, especially partial to tones ranging between soft rose and purple-violet, to olive-green and steel-blue for bushes and trees, to underpainting with a strong brown not always appropriate to the concrete object depicted. He had no hesitation in combining the sweep of wash drawing with the most precise miniature-like details, and it

15. MEMENTO MEI. 1505. Charcoal drawing.
British Museum, London

did not matter much to him if houses lay in sun or shadow.

Certain watercolors are often attributed to the time following this first journey, among them *Mills on a River* (W 113), *House on an Island in a Pond* (W 115) later incorporated into the engraving *The Madonna with the Monkey* (B 42), and *Pond in the Woods* (page 61). It is far more likely that, like the *Linden Tree on a Bastion* painted on vellum (W 63) and *Three Linden Trees* (W 64), they had already been done in Nuremberg. This would explain why they differ so much in style from the *Quarries* (W 106–9), of which one was later used for the background of the *St. Jerome in Penitence* engraving and which were certainly done after the artist had returned home.

Because of the marked development in use of perspective, the *View of Nuremberg* (W 116) must belong to the time shortly before 1500, whereas the *Hamlet of Kalckreuth* (W 118), with its virtually cubist treatment of space and its play of light against dark, can presumably be placed in the first years of the new century.

PAINTINGS

With his very first painting, the portrait of his father from 1490 (page 53), Dürer appears as a fully formed artist still very much tied to the Nuremberg tradition. And yet, as early as the self-portrait of 1493 (page 55) —the first in all of Europe—there is something entirely new and different. This was painted on his wanderings and sent back home, possibly as a pledge for the matchmaking his father was carrying on for him.

Although the St. Dominic altarpiece (page 59) survives in fragments only, it reveals the great breadth of talent the young painter already possessed in religious art.

In Venice, unsuspected possibilities opened wide before him. The fact that he was traveling abroad probably explains the small dimensions of three early panels, the *Ecce Homo* (page 57), the *St. Jerome in the Wilderness* (page 67), and the *St. Christopher* now in Dessau. In the two pictures of saints there is proof of his newly awakened feeling for nature and landscape.

Upon his return to Nuremberg began the association with the Elector Frederick the Wise, which resulted in the portrait (page 69) and the altarpieces of the Passion and the Madonna, both now in Dresden (page 71). The only recently discovered *Madonna and Child* (fig. 7), which is currently on the art market, must come from but slightly later.

The date of 1497 is given for the two portraits of women of the Fürleger family, known only through copies and two copperplate engravings by Hollar (fig. 6), as well as for the second portrait of his father, who, in seven years, had aged visibly (page 73). From 1498 come the dazzling *Self-Portrait* (frontispiece), whose composition is echoed in the Bergamo *St. Sebastian*, and also the Paumgartner altarpiece with *The Nativity* as its central panel (page 77; fig. 11) and —an unheard-of innovation—life-size portraits of the donor's sons depicted as saints on the wings (page 79). To the same time belongs the *Haller Madonna*, now in Washington, painted for a branch of the Nuremberg Haller family, which has on the back of the panel the amusing *Lot and His Daughters* (page 75), whose attractions outweigh for most people those of the principal picture.

The following year, 1499, was a year for portraits: the *Oswolt Krel* with coats of arms on the hinged side panels (in Munich) and the *Hans* and *Elsbeth Tucher*, respectively in Weimar and Cassel. An absolutely un-

paralleled achievement is the *Self-Portrait* of 1500 (page 83), and the *Portrait of a Young Man* of the same year scarcely lags behind in excellence (page 85). Of the two *Lamentations over the Dead Christ*, the one for the Glimm family (page 81) was done in 1500, that for the Holzschuher family (in Nuremberg) may date from one or two years earlier.

The approach applied in these large-scale works— circumscribed, clearly defined surfaces loosely filled in—was then abandoned. Only once did Dürer paint an antique mythological motif, the *Hercules and the Stymphalian Birds* (in Nuremberg), a tempera painting whose condition is now not very satisfactory. Apart from the small *Salvator Mundi* altarpiece in New York (page 89), with its side panels of which only one survives (the *St. Onophrius* in Bremen), four years were to pass before there would once again be a larger work: the so-called Jabach or Three Kings altarpiece whose central panel with *The Adoration of the Magi* is in Florence (page 93), the two wings with *Joseph and Joachim* (page 95) and *Simon and Lazarus* in Munich, the shutters with *Job and His Wife* and *Drummer and Piper* (page 97) in Frankfurt and Cologne respectively. In these, Dürer's color, which until then had been tonal and muted, became instead fresh and bright.

In the course of the second sojourn in Italy were produced, in 1505, the *Portrait of a Venetian Woman* (page 99) and, in the following year, *The Madonna of the Rose Garlands* (page 103; fig. 16) which unfortunately is badly deteriorated, as is *The Madonna with the Siskin* in Berlin. But there are also the splendidly preserved *Madonna before Arched Walls* in the Capuchin monastery at Bagnacavallo near Ravenna (page 101), the Windsor Castle *Portrait of a Man* (the sitter reappears among the personages in *The Madonna of the Rose Garlands*), and a similar, truly enchanting painting of 1507 in Vienna. Without date is the *Portrait of a Woman* in Berlin, which many scholars have attempted to identify with the artist's wife without, it must be said, much justification.

Back in Nuremberg, in 1507 Dürer painted the two large panels with Adam and Eve (page 105) and, as another commission from Frederick the Wise, *The Martyrdom of the Ten Thousand Christians under King Sapor* dated 1508, now in Vienna.

Long and arduous work went into the altarpiece commissioned by the merchant Jakob Heller, which was finally completed in 1509. Tragically, this was destroyed in the fire in the Munich Residence in 1729, and its capital importance is testified to now only by

16. THE MADONNA OF THE ROSE GARLANDS. 1506. *National Gallery, Prague*

a large number of very beautiful preparatory studies. A small, badly deteriorated *Holy Family* in Rotterdam bears the same date.

Dürer's most important well-preserved painting with numerous figures is *The Adoration of the Trinity*, the so-called All Saints altarpiece, dated 1511 (page 107; fig. 22). It is a radiant work with exquisite jewel-like coloring, its brilliance heightened by the gold employed in the costumes. Surely this is how the lost Heller altarpiece and the damaged *Madonna of the Rose Garlands* must have been. Dark shadows are banished from the artist's vocabulary, nothing is allowed to dim the natural luster of the figures and objects: "You must paint a red thing," wrote Dürer, "so that it is red all over, the same with other colors, and yet they must be made to appear modeled as if in relief." Cézanne said much the same thing when he rated *moduler* higher than *modeler*.

17. HEAD OF AN APOSTLE (study for the HELLER ALTARPIECE).
1508. Brush drawing. *Albertina, Vienna*

18. FEMALE NUDE SEEN FROM THE REAR.
1506. Brush drawing. *State Museums, Berlin-Dahlem*

To be considered merely as routine commissioned works are the two portraits of the Emperors Charlemagne and Sigismund ordered by the Nuremberg town council for the depository in the Schopper House on the market square, where the Imperial treasures were displayed each year for a few days after Easter. On the other hand, the *Madonna and Child with a Pear* of 1512 (page 109) brought to a head all of the new techniques and discoveries Dürer had acquired in Italy and of which he was justly proud. The *Portrait of a Young Man* against a red background can be dated somewhere around 1514 (page 113).

Traces of the artificial technique of construction according to theoretical principles are somewhat too

evident still in the Munich *Madonna with a Carnation.* The Johannes Dorsch portrait now in Washington seems to be in poor condition. However, the two *Apostles* in Florence belong among Dürer's most beautiful, most powerful and deeply felt paintings (page 117). In the portrait of Michael Wolgemut (page 115) the artist gave expression to his gratitude and high esteem for his former master who was then in his eighties, whereas once again there is something too much of theoretical artifice in the Munich *Lucretia.* But the *Virgin in Prayer* (page 119) and the *Madonna and Child with St. Anne* (page 123), both from 1519, are splendid works, and the deep respect Dürer felt for Emperor Maximilian I is brought out in the two portraits now in Nuremberg (page 121) and Vienna. It must have been around 1520 that he did the portrait of Jakob Fugger in tempera on canvas (page 125).

Of the many portraits in oil recorded in the Netherlands travel journal, only a few seem to have survived: the *Bernhard von Resten* (page 129), the Boston *Lorenz Sterck*, which is in bad condition, the *Jobst Planckfelt* (page 131), and, presumably, the poorly preserved portrait of the latter's wife, now in Toledo, Ohio. One of the finest products of the Netherlands voyage is the *St. Jerome* (page 127). All of these paintings reveal a pictorial refinement due in part to the considerable influence on Dürer that artists like Massys exercised, in part to the atmosphere itself of the Netherlands.

The year 1526 saw the creation of two powerful works, the portraits of Hieronymus Holzschuher (page 135) and Jakob Muffel (page 137), along with that of Johann Kleeberger, now in Vienna, and a *Madonna and Child* (page 133) which turned out to be the last picture Dürer painted in honor of the Virgin.

Dürer's creative life was concluded with a crowning achievement, *The Four Apostles* (pages 139 and 141).

If the notion is still rife that Albrecht Dürer was without question a great artist but not equally great as a painter, the master himself was at least in part responsible for it. On September 8, 1506, he wrote from Venice to his friend Pirckheimer, "And I also gave the lie to the painters here who say I am good at engraving but don't really know what to do with colors." And then, to Jakob Heller in Frankfurt, he wrote on August 26, 1509, "Such slow and painstaking exertions simply do not pay off in the end, so I have made up my mind to stick to engraving from now on."

Both statements have over and over again been misinterpreted. For one thing, it must not be overlooked that our painter himself was finally able to win the respect of his Venetian colleagues and that, in any event, the opinions of artists about one another must, by the nature of things, always be subjective. In Venice, what was prized was the painterly approach, the exploitation of color in and for itself, and so it was only natural that the Venetians judged the Germans harshly. But too much should not be made out of this, since they were no less critical of their Florentine rivals.

As for Dürer's second assertion, it has to do only with the commercial rewards of painting. It was made in connection with his remark that he could dash off in a year a great pile of run-of-the-mill paintings of

19. THE PENITENT. 1510. Woodcut

the sort that paid off well and quickly, whereas anything out of the ordinary simply was not profitable, since it took too much time to do.

Anyone who parrots such misinterpretations of the artist's own words is wrongfully substituting his own scale of values for Dürer's, and ends up by pronouncing as arbitrary judgments as someone who thinks he has said something when he asserts that Richard Wagner made music but Johann Sebastian Bach did not. Instead, one should see things the other way around and marvel at what fascinating, truly painterly creations Dürer was able to achieve with such simple means, with drawing taking its part as one technique among others. And yet, we cannot doubt that he must have been entirely sincere in what he said, since after completing *The Adoration of the Trinity* a full fifteen years went by in which he never turned his hand to any painting in large dimensions or with numerous figures.

COPPERPLATE ENGRAVINGS

In Nuremberg before Dürer, no one had done copperplate engravings. Dürer learned the technique during his youthful travels in Alsace, not from Martin Schongauer himself, who was the greatest master of the time, but from Schongauer's brother and pupils. However, his first engravings seem to date only from after his return from his first stay in Italy. This is understandable: even a Dürer needed some time to master the technique of cutting into a polished copperplate with a graver or burin that digs a furrow like a ploughshare to make an image which, when printed, will come out reversed from left to right. It is of note that the earliest engravings are shaded on the left, and it was not until around 1500 that the light was made to flow from left to right in conformity with what, in the Occident at least, is the natural course of the eye. Like woodcuts, copperplate engravings involve the transfer to the plate of a fully worked-out preliminary drawing.

Unlike Schongauer, whose conceptions were entirely religious, Dürer with his highly subtle and finely detailed technique greatly enlarged the domain of subject matter open to the print, introducing nudes, both male and female, landscapes, allegories—all the vast realm of fantasy. As proof, there are the great achievements of his early years: the *St. Eustace* from shortly before 1500, the *Nemesis* from soon after, and the *Adam and Eve* of 1504.

The *St. Eustace* (fig. 8) recounts a medieval legend of magic and miracle. Attended by his horse and by five brilliantly drawn greyhounds handsomely disposed across the surface of the print, the Saint kneels in a wondrously beautiful wooded place with a splendid castle in the far background. The miracle of the Crucifix which appeared to him between the antlers of the stag he was pursuing is entirely spiritualized, an experience transcending the merely visible.

The *Great Fortune* (which was preceded by a *Small Fortune*), also called *Nemesis*, is a heavy-bodied, winged, and naked woman with swelling belly and massive thighs. Trailing her drapery behind her, she bestrides a sphere which soars above a mountainous landscape (Klausen, in fact) which is already touched by nightfall. She carries in one hand a bridle to curb presumptuous spirits, in the other a goblet for those who win victory in life. The entire image is so steeped in perceptive observation that the allegory itself takes second place.

The engraving *Adam and Eve* (fig. 12), whose prototype can be found in the earlier *Apollo and Diana*, sums up everything the artist learned from his nude studies and constructions of the preceding years. He conceived the first humans as something quintessential, the eternal Idea as it came from the hand of God, without for all that in the least slighting their individual characterization. To accomplish this at the close of the Middle Ages which had proscribed all nudity, was an act of unheard-of intrepidity. One senses the gentle blush suffusing Eve, while Adam glories in the possession of his strong-muscled sinewy nude body. His tight-coiled hair is like the foliage roundabout, metal cut out by the sharp chisel. To have seen this engraving in a first-rate printing such as all great public collections possess is never to forget what a true masterwork can be.

From the start, Dürer turned out a vast number of engravings in both large and small formats. Among them are true genre pictures, glimpses of everyday life like the *Peasant Couple Dancing* of 1514 and the *Peasants at Market* of 1519 (fig. 42) with their penetrating social criticism and realism, but there are also purely ornamental images of coats of arms and emblems such as

20. THE BEARING OF THE CROSS.
From the Small Woodcut Passion. 1509

28

the *Lion Escutcheon with Cock* and the *Escutcheon with Death's-Head* of 1503.

The sixteen sheets of the Engraved Passion done between 1508 and 1513, preceded by the profoundly moving *Small Crucifixion* of 1508, strongly suggest contact with Grünewald. They make it evident that prints such as these were intended for connoisseurs and art-lovers more than for the mass of the faithful. Even the person who recoils from the unstinted sympathy with the sufferings of Christ which these images aim at must be awed by their composition and superb accomplishment as engravings. For us today, what is most impressive is the mastery with which Dürer conveys, for instance, the silky shimmer of the drapery of one of the tormentors of Christ, or the humorous odd originality of the beribboned Till Eulenspiegel-like cupbearer who pours water into Pilate's basin (fig. 26), or the mocking figure in *Ecce Homo* whose monumental character led Andrea del Sarto to copy it in one of his frescoes.

Just as the music of Johann Sebastian Bach touches deeply even those without religious convictions, so too can they be stirred by *The Holy Cloth of Veronica*, done in 1513 (fig. 25), with its wonderful soaring angels of lamentation, so different one from the other. Here Dürer achieved the ultimate formulation of his personal interpretation of Christ, of Christ as Man.

There are fourteen engraved Madonnas by Dürer, and they bear witness to his great powers of invention. Some are fervent, others intimate, German to the core or Italianate, simple maidens or resplendent Queens of Heaven. In the last ones he did he arrived at a type of blocklike figure sturdy as a servant girl.

Without any apparent reasonable explanation, suddenly shortly before the middle of the second decade of the sixteenth century, after having virtually given up individual woodcuts, Dürer produced the three great master engravings on which so much of his fame rests. In the *Knight, Death, and Devil* of 1513 (fig. 27), to which the *St. George* of 1508 was a prelude, Dürer wished to depict the Christian knight who acknowledges neither fear nor retreat. Nietzsche, who always kept a print of it at hand, called the Knight "imperturbable and yet without hope." To be sure, the man —who has a striking resemblance to Savonarola—is encased in armor. His horse derives from those by Leonardo da Vinci and from Dürer's 1505 engravings of the *Small Horse*, which is still very much constructed on theoretical principles, and the *Great Horse*, which is much more modeled after nature. No more than

21. THE REST ON THE FLIGHT INTO EGYPT. 1511. Pen drawing. *State Museums, Berlin-Dahlem*

its master is the horse in its proud progress deterred by the wretched bugbear of Death on his dilapidated nag or by the ludicrous Devil with pig-snout and scimitar-horn.

The *Melencolia I* (fig. 30) and the *St. Jerome in His Study* (fig. 29) were done in the following year, 1514. In the former, the winged, brooding woman, heavy and apathetic, squats in the lower right of the picture in a dress of silk and a woolen blouse, crowned with a garland and toying listlessly with the compass she holds in her lap. The womanly figure should not really be interpreted in the modern sense of melancholy, as the disconsolate mood of one sick of life or despairing of it. Rather, it is to be taken as the symbol of a specific psychological quality possessed by men whose talents turn toward intellectual creation, a notion which goes back to Aristotle and Ficino. It has been proposed that the Roman numeral I in the inscription is evidence that Dürer had in mind, as a companion piece for this benign melancholy, that other melancholy, evil in cause and effects, which stems from a deep sickness of the soul. The cherub seated on a millstone and scribbling on a slate, the dog curled up in a ball, the enormous cube of stone, the many tools scattered about the ground, the sphere, hourglass, bell, and magic square—each is a detail in itself and yet all are united in the wan light which, contrary to Dürer's custom, seeps in from the right (in the sky there is a comet and a rainbow around the moon poised above the horizontals of a landscape of sea and shore).

With the third master engraving, *St. Jerome in His Study*, for which the *Nativity* of 1504 was in a way a preparation, Dürer seems to have sought to depict yet another aspect of the way men live their lives. Clearly, what he had in mind here was the quiet joy in existence, the pure peace that comes from God. In a secluded wood-paneled room the Saint sits before a small lectern, completely absorbed in the ardor of writing. The sun pours in through the bull's-eye glass and casts a pattern on the deep recesses of the window niche. Even the death's-head on the ledge does not strike a jarring note, and the large shape of the cardinal's hat hanging on the wall as well as the giant gourd suspended from the ceiling play their part in creating an impression of tranquility and peaceful retirement, further enhanced by the enemy animals which lie down together. At the threshold a dog lies trustingly asleep alongside a lion which has thrust aside all recollection of the nature of the beast. The kingly animal watches over the quiet of the room, forever grateful to the Saint who once removed a painful thorn from his paw.

In 1514 Dürer began a series of Apostles but completed no more than *Thomas* and *Paul*, figures glowing with fervor. Not until 1523 did he add *Bartholomew* and *Simon*, both of a fully mature statuesque quality, and *Philip* (fig. 41), which Dürer himself inscribed as 1526 although it was done three years earlier. Two engravings of St. Christopher were executed in 1521.

Earlier, in 1519, Dürer engraved *St. Anthony before a City* (fig. 36). With consummate clarity the silhouette of the crouching Capuchin stretches out in front of a city towering up in the background. Here the artist reached new heights in his powers of conception and, interestingly enough, did not hesitate to incorporate in this engraving landscape sketches done long before in Innsbruck and Trent which he had already utilized in the drawing *Pupila Augusta* (W 153).

Great success rewarded his *Small Cardinal* (Albrecht of Brandenburg, Archbishop of Mainz) in that same year, 1519. We know that the princely prelate reserved two hundred prints for himself and showered gifts on the artist, two hundred gold guilders as well as twenty ells of damask for a coat.

This led to a commission to engrave the *Great Cardinal* in 1523, followed by other portraits in the same large format, among them those of Frederick the Wise and Willibald Pirckheimer (fig. 40) in 1524 and Philipp Melanchthon and Erasmus in 1526.

A large-format *Crucifixion*, prepared by very beautiful detail studies from the early 1520s, never got beyond the stage of planning. It might well have been one of the finest of all the engravings.

At various times Dürer also tried his hand at drypoint and etching, for which steel plates were used, and he was, in fact, one of the first to experiment with those media in such outstanding prints as the *St. Jerome* of 1512 and the *Cannon* of 1518 (fig. 31).

22. THE ALL SAINTS ALTARPIECE (THE ADORATION OF THE TRINITY). 1511. *Kunsthistorisches Museum, Vienna*

23. THE TAKING OF CHRIST. From the Large Woodcut Passion. 1510

WOODCUTS

In Dürer's time the woodcut was not a personal, first-hand kind of art like the copperplate engraving. The artist did the original drawing on the woodblock, but someone else, the block-cutter, did the actual work of chiseling out the furrows of the image to be printed. Only very rarely did Dürer himself use the carving tools. To do more would have been impossible, for in his day the cutting of a block was a long and tedious task better left to specialized craftsmen, most of whom were joiners with particular training as form-cutters. The names of some of Dürer's assistants have come down to us, among them Hieronymus Andreae.

Dürer was no more than a boy when he was set to learning the craft of woodcutting and blockprinting in the workshop of his godfather Anton Koberger, the most eminent printer of his day who had to his credit some of the most important publications of the Nuremberg book trade, including the *Schatzbehalter* and Schedel's *Weltchronik*. Among those who worked for Koberger were Pleydenwurff and Wolgemut, to the latter of whom Dürer was apprenticed at fifteen. It is not improbable that the young Dürer had a share in the designs turned out in the workshop.

His first woodcuts date from his wanderyears in Basel and Strassburg, where he worked for various publishers. A great many wood blocks for an edition of Terence's comedies have survived in Basel, all prepared with drawings but never cut, and there is one with Dürer's signature in full. Besides these, he was no doubt involved in the illustrations for Sebastian Brant's *Ship of Fools* and for the *Ritter vom Turn*. His career was well launched with the Apocalypse series, on which he worked for some years before Koberger published it in 1498 in book form in Nuremberg.

The fifteen large-format sheets illustrate the visions of St. John who, banished to the island of Patmos, underwent revelations of great catastrophes menacing the world, and recorded them with passionate conviction. For Dürer, this, his greatest work, had special meaning: in it he sought to explain and to bridle the terrible fear of death which oppressed mankind as the fatal year of 1500 approached when destruction had been prophesied to the world. The series opens with the martyrdom of the Saint in a vat of oil in the presence of the Emperor Domitian, whom Dürer, no doubt recalling what he had seen in Venice, depicted as a Turkish pasha enthroned before a grotesquely

24. HOLY FAMILY WITH JOACHIM AND ST. ANNE.
1511. Woodcut

gesticulating populace (1). Then one sees John fallen on his knees before the apparition of the Son of Man and surrounded by seven golden candlesticks symbolizing "the seven churches which are in Asia" to which the Saint's mission was to take him (2). On the next sheet, one of the twenty-four Elders of the Apocalypse consoles the weeping Saint and shows him the Lamb of God that alone is "worthy to take the book, and to open the seals thereof" (3). The white, red, and black horses and their terrifying cavaliers released by the opening of the seals are joined by the "pale horse, pale rider" of Death to thunder over "the fourth part of the earth" which must be destroyed (4). This is the most celebrated of the Apocalypse woodcuts (fig. 9).

25. THE HOLY CLOTH OF VERONICA. 1513. Engraving

Dürer must have chosen the large format for the series because he recognized that such visions in which the entire age believed and whose fulfillment was awaited with fear and trembling must be depicted with the fullest impact that only large dimensions could give. But it was not alone the extravagant imagery of these fantasies exploding in mighty bursts of lines that gave these pictures a force such as to spread, suddenly, Dürer's fame throughout the civilized world: they represent also the perfect synthesis of a typically Northern imagination with the plasticity and precision the artist had learned from Italy.

Probably from about the same time are some separate sheets in large format and a few from the Large Passion, most notably the *Lamentation of Christ*. Here the background is made to rise steeply above the foreground figures. Accuracy of perspective was sacrificed in the interest of a more graphic and more powerful presentation.

Then "the mighty men, and every bondman, and every free man, hid themselves in the dens and in the rocks of the mountains" (5). Next come four virile angels to hold back the four winds of the earth and "an hundred and forty and four thousand of all the tribes" are "sealed" (6), and the saved chant a mighty hymn of praise (7). And still the plagues and punishments go on: seven angels sound their trumpets, spreading fear and terror over the earth (8), and the Angels of the Euphrates wreak punishment on mankind (9). John then devours bodily the little book received from the angel's hand, signifying that yet more duties were to be laid on him, and this esoteric symbolism, so difficult to communicate, is convincingly expressed by Dürer (10). Thereupon appears "a woman clothed with the sun"—the Virgin Mary—pursued by a horrific dragon, but her Son is caught up and rescued by God (11). High above, in the clouds, the Archangel Michael wars against the Dragon (12). The Great Whore of Babylon astride a blasphemous beast is adored by the richly attired kings of the earth, but her city is delivered up to the flames (13). The taking and binding of Satan is not depicted by Dürer, but in the last plate the Devil is locked away in the pit for a thousand years (15), preceding which, however, other dragons and the false beast with two horns like a lamb are worshiped by the great and foolish of the earth (14).

34

26. PILATE WASHING HIS HANDS. From the Engraved Passion. 1512

Concurrently with the similar stylistic change in his drawings, the Life of Mary series reveals most clearly Dürer's new orientation toward the world, though the struggle to master scientific perspective was not yet fully won. These woodcuts are relaxed, cheerful, full of bright sun, and we take pleasure in the joyous bustle in the room where St. Anne gives birth to the Virgin. The *Joachim and St. Anne Meeting at the Golden Gate* of 1504 is conceived with all the breadth of gesture the scene calls for (fig. 10), and the *Visitation* is wholly without hint of the tragic destiny which awaits the children with whom both women are heavy.

The two scenes from the life of John the Baptist, done in 1510 and 1511, and the *Penitent* of 1510 (fig. 19) reveal a hitherto unknown feeling for clear disposition of space and tectonic exploitation of the cube.

In those same years Dürer completed the series of the Large Passion and the Life of Mary and published them along with the Apocalypse and the Small Wood-cut Passion, which contains many more episodes than the Large Passion. In 1511 appeared the *Holy Family* (fig. 24), a festive sun-drenched picture in large dimensions, and also the monumental *Trinity* whose composition became the source of inspiration for even an El Greco. After these, however, he tended to do woodcuts only as special commissions, in particular for Emperor Maximilian, the margins of whose prayer book he decorated with drawings (fig. 33) from which woodcuts were made later. He also collaborated in 1515 on the Emperor's *Triumphal Arch*, a project somewhat grotesque in conception but amply justified by Dürer's brilliantly designed contributions. The *Triumphal Procession* for the Emperor was prepared in 1518 but not published until 1522. As a great master Dürer also undertook the gold-plate portrait of the Emperor, which was not brought out until after Maximilian's death on January 12, 1519, after which some copies were made.

Dürer's production of woodcuts, which had begun

27. KNIGHT, DEATH, AND DEVIL. 1513. Engraving

so prolifically, ended with merely isolated pieces, the portrait of Ulrich Varnbüler in 1522 and *The Last Supper* in 1523 (fig. 43). And yet, in the latter he achieved what he had admired so much in the Italians, a work truly "after the manner of the Ancients."

35

For Dürer the alpha and omega of art was the human being, male or female, in all his God-given beauty, and this notion in itself was entirely alien to the Middle Ages. In man Dürer saw the image of God in a comparable way as the Greeks imagined their gods as men. But what was easily understandable in ancient times, that a God should be beautiful, seemed in the waning Middle Ages scarcely possible of rational explanation. Dürer saw things otherwise: "Just as the Ancients attributed to their false god Apollo the most beautiful traits of a man, so do we wish to employ the same measures for Christ our Lord, the most beautiful being in all the world. And as they depicted Venus as the most beautiful of women, so too—but chastely—do we aspire to portray the most pure Virgin Mary, God's mother." To Dürer, "beautiful" and "godlike" meant one and the same thing: "made in proportionate measure."

Very early, it seems, Dürer came to take it for granted that there was a single, unique godlike proportion. This was a point of view to which he came early in his first sojourn in Italy, and he knew already that this law of proportions was something stonemasons and master builders respected in their daily work. In one of the first drafts of the dedication to Pirckheimer of his book on human proportion, he made clear his interest in the whole question. There he refers to the Venetian painter Jacopo de' Barbari who settled in Nuremberg in 1500 but with whom Dürer had become acquainted many years before when, as he says of himself, "I was still very young and hadn't a notion of things like that." Jacopo, Dürer explains, "let me see a male and a female figure which he had drawn according to a canon of proportions"—which were, in other words, not imitated from nature but "constructed"—but the older man was reluctant to give away the secret of how this was done. For his part, and by his own statement, Dürer clung to the lesson of Vitruvius, architect of the Emperor Augustus, "who describes somewhat the proportions of a man," reckoning those proportions as certain fractions of the body's mass. Later, however, Dürer conformed to the canon proposed by Leon Battista Alberti, but in his mature years conceded that, in point of fact, many different types exist, each of which is constructed according to certain measures, that is, possesses its own innate unity of proportions. This means that once

again beauty partakes of the subjective, though it still remains dependent on stylistic unity: "The parts must be commensurate one to another, linked in a specific harmonious relationship which must remain constant throughout all the parts of a body." Principles like these go back to Leonardo da Vinci and, before him, to Alberti.

Alberti's concept of *concinnitas* was based on the same phenomenon, and was summed up thus by Leonardo: "Every part of a whole is proportionate to the whole." In his own down-to-earth language (of which no translation can capture the racy directness) Dürer expressed the same idea: "It is more fitting that a thick-set strong naked figure should be of a firmer stamp and heftier than a naked figure that is scrawny, skinny, and more flimsy. One part should not be fatter, another skinnier, as it would be if you made thick legs and lean arms and suchlike contradictions, or a fat front and a meager behind or vice versa."

In this he shows that he has learned the lesson of nature which, however varied its bases may be, always retains a certain stylistic unity. It is in this way that must be understood his dictum which so many people misinterpret by turning it into an all-embracing generalization: "For truly art is contained within nature, and he who can seize it has got it." His attitude is, in fact, liberal enough, since he also says, "It is not always necessary to measure every single thing, because once you have made your art your own, you can depend on the judgment of your eye." If the artist has learned the true science of proportions and is accustomed to applying it, any image he wishes can be turned out and he has no need to fuss over its proportions in every single case.

Dürer's theoretical constructions are for the most part in the form of drawings (in the Dresden sketchbook). Apart from a few unimportant examples, in works intended for the public Dürer simply brushed aside all theoretical considerations or, at least, skillfully concealed the underlying construction. Thausing put it nicely: "The theory and teachings of art are, in Dürer, not so much the vehicle as the fruit of his creative activity." It remains true, however, that almost unconsciously they led Dürer himself to recognition of the significance of relationships within a plane surface, to greater clarity in form, and to an extraordinary security in drawing the nude.

Melanchthon is responsible for the notion that Dürer in his youth delighted most in depicting monstrous or bizarre figures, so that it was not until his late years

28. DÜRER'S MOTHER. 1514. Charcoal drawing. *State Museums, Berlin-Dahlem*

29. ST. JEROME IN HIS STUDY. 1514. Engraving

his direction with great attention to every detail: he chose the finest type faces and saw to it that they were printed with utmost technical perfection and provided with woodcuts relevant to the subject as well as many illustrations of nudes constructed according to his theory and for which he furnished the drawings. Only at the end of the treatise on geometry are there two (four in the 1538 edition) pictures of purely artistic character included as examples of perspective. As late as a century after his death, according to Wölfflin, Dürer was still almost as renowned for his writings as for his art works. In 1532, in the commentary he wrote for the Latin translation of the *Proportionslehre*, Camerarius stressed that Dürer was the first since antiquity to elevate *praxis*—utility—into a scientific system (*quod ad artem et rationem usum revocarat*).

The theoretical writings comprise four books:

1. *Underweysung der Messung mit dem Zirckel und Richt- scheyt in Linien, Ebenen und ganzen Körpern*, Nuremberg, 1525, Koberger.

This "Instruction in Measurement with Compass and Ruler of Lines, Surfaces, and Solid Bodies" treats of mathematical figures as Original Ideas instilled by God into the human intellect, and its orientation is philosophical and religious. It deals with geometrical figures, curves even of higher form, and stereometric structures with special reference to what an artist needs to know about them. In addition, there is an explanation of how to construct letters in both Antique style and Gothic Black Letter. The chief sources are the classical authors Euclid and Vitruvius (Dürer had acquired a Euclid in Venice in 1507, which can be seen in the Wolfenbüttel library complete with his signature and memorandum of purchase). To these he added the Italians L. B. Alberti and Luca Pacioli whose *De divina proportione* is translated erroneously in German by the too-general title *On the Golden Section*. There is one more source, a *Geometria* published in German in Nuremberg in 1483/84. This is a small volume from which Dürer could have learned very little, but it is worthy of remark because it contains a geometrical diagram for a spiked jousting helmet, a subject Dürer was later to use for himself. Interestingly enough, Dürer's *Underweysung* contains as an illustration a project for a column to commemorate the Peasants' War. Though it is of questionable taste and highly problematical as an art work, it shows that, unlike Luther in this, Dürer, "that sober-minded and thoroughly upright spirit, still unequivocally took the side of the

that he began to observe nature and attempt to imitate it properly, thereby coming to understand at last that art's greatest glory lies precisely in such simplicity. Alberti summarized this idea in *Neque nimi neque addi aliquid posse* – "Beauty is a specific harmony of all parts subject to certain laws, and is such that one cannot add to it or take away from it or alter it in any way without making it less pleasing." This is what Goethe meant when, in Rome, on September 6, 1787, he declared: "Where Necessity is, there is God." Dürer's painstaking step-by-step working-out of his projects for the *Virgin and Saints* during 1521 and 1522 and for *The Four Apostles* is an excellent example of this creed.

Dürer was much concerned about posterity. He was convinced that his scientific views could be of use to future generations, and resolved therefore to set them down in book form. The books were prepared under defeated party after the complete collapse of the peasants' revolt," as Wilhelm Fraenger put it. There are also, it is true, other interpretations (Panofsky, Wittkower).

2. *Die Befestigungslehre*, Nuremberg, 1527.

The book on fortification of cities, castles, and open places grew out of the need for protection against peasant uprisings and Turkish invasions, and cities like Nuremberg and Strassburg put Dürer's plans to practical use. The book contains admirably drawn and executed woodcuts of ground plans and elevations for fortifications, and the first edition included the large woodcut *Siege of a Fortress*.

3. *Die Proportionslehre*, Nuremberg, 1528.

Originally planned as a comprehensive manual of painting, the *Four Books on Human Proportion* did not come out until after Dürer's death. It is his major achievement in theoretical writing and was soon translated into six languages including Latin; there was an English edition in 1690. In his book on painting, Pacheco, the teacher of Velázquez, still recommends that young artists should learn female anatomy from the woodcuts in Dürer's book rather than from live models. Here, too, Dürer's theory derives from Vitruvius and the Italians (Alberti's *De pictura* was published in German translation in 1511 in Nuremberg).

Vitruvius took as his basis the length of the human body, which he then divided according to the Golden Section in order to arrive at the correct measures for individual parts such as the arm, foot, hand, or head.

Like the Greeks, Vitruvius' interests embraced animals, plants, and sculpture as well as architecture. Dürer carried the program further through his investigations of how foreshortening and elongation are related to the standard measure. This led him to formulate stylistic criteria which allow for both diversity and unity and which are applicable also to overly slender or excessively developed bodies and their positioning and movement within a space. The book contains many woodcut constructions, projections, front and side views, and volumetrically simplified diagrams of the human body which Dürer prepared merely as illustrations without any higher artistic aim.

4. *Speis der Malerknaben*.

In this work, which might be rendered as *Food for Thought for Apprentice Painters*, Dürer attempted to sum up his own theoretical and practical experience in

30. MELENCOLIA I. 1514. Engraving

31. THE CANNON. 1518. Etching

32. SIX NUDES. 1515. Pen drawing.
Städel Institute, Frankfurt am Main

the form of a textbook for those "who wish to learn and to arrive at a higher understanding of art." Left unfinished, it was never published, and all that survives of it are preliminary drafts of the text and prefaces.

The book aims to prevent talented artists from growing up, as Dürer puts it, "thoughtless." Mere practice and manual skill are not enough, he says. Rather, the artist should have a thorough education in all aspects of his art. How deep was Dürer's sympathy for his fellow man is obvious when he declares that he writes "to give comfort to that gifted lad who loves art more than silver and gold." He recommends that such a student be decently housed and fed and protected from the wiles of women, neither seeing them naked nor touching them. Also he champions the notion that "a superlative artist should be richly rewarded for his art, and no money can ever compensate him in full. For indeed, the world waits often two or three hundred years without a truly gifted master turning up."

Lectio tertia.

Uasi cedrus exaltata
sum in libano:et quasi
cypressus in monte syon Qua
si palma exaltata sum in ca
des:et quasi plantatio rose in
iericho Quasi oliua speciosa
in campis:et quasi platan⁹ exalta
ta sum iurta aquas in plateis
sicut cynamomum et balsa
mum aromatizans odorem
dedi Quasi mirrha electa de
di suauitate odoris Tu aute
domine Respon Felir naq

1515

33. Page with marginal decoration in Emperor Maximilian's Prayer Book. 1515. *Staatsbibliothek, Munich*

34. THE HARBOR AT ANTWERP. 1520. Pen drawing. *Albertina, Vienna*

35. ST. PETER AND STUDIES IN CONSTRUCTION OF HEADS. From the Dresden Sketchbook. 1519. Pen drawing.
Saxon State Library, Dresden

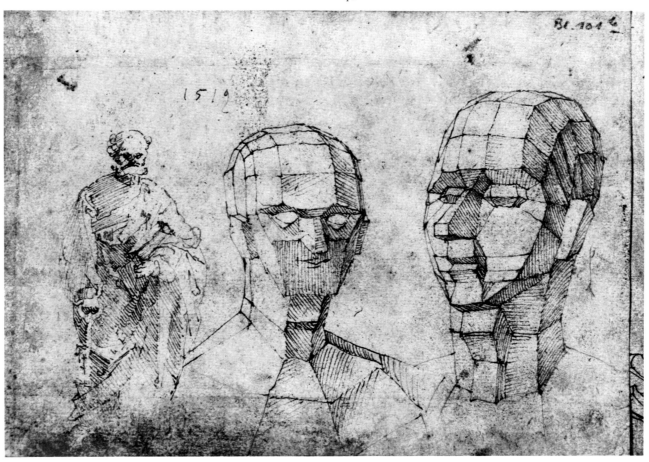

MAN AND ARTIST

We know Dürer better than most great artists of the past because he left us not only his art works but also writings of many kinds. Though at first sight everything about him seems open and clear, much still needs explaining, and especially to men of today.

It is of note that his deep religious feeling—an inborn inheritance from the Middle Ages which viewed nature herself as an enemy—was nevertheless linked with a consuming passion to grasp the entire visible world. That is why he defined painting as the art of portraying on a flat surface (board, paper, canvas, and the like) some particular thing chosen at will from the vast realm of visible things and portraying it in such a way and with such a suggestion of relief that the eye is tricked into taking it for real. In this, there is a radical break with the relative flatness and indifference to space of the High Gothic, and it was a development which had come about only shortly before Dürer's time. For close on to half a millennium now men have taken this achievement for granted, and it is only at the present time that our ideas of what a picture can be are changing. For Dürer what mattered most was that art be *new:* "Only a dried-up mind has no confidence in itself to find its way to something further, and so drags on in the same old path content to imitate others and without the gumption to think ahead for itself." The art of painting "serves the Church and conveys the message of the sufferings of Christ, but it is also the means to preserve the likenesses of men after their deaths. And only through painting have men learned to comprehend the vastness of the earth and seas and stars."

No less important to him was the need to base the artist's activity on conscious understanding: "He who works without understanding works harder than the man who knows what he is doing." He found that in the Germanic countries there were a great many talented young fellows, but they had been left to grow up in ignorance "like a wild unpruned tree." Understanding must be developed along with manual skill, so that the hand can do what the reasoning mind commands. Before going on to study anything else, the young artist must learn to portray everything in proper proportions, and not only human figures— "a man, a woman, a child, a horse." As is logical, he places great worth on mathematics and geometry, since by means of construction they guarantee correct proportions: "He who works according to geometry and reveals the underlying truth makes the whole world believe in what he does.... Beauty, which is given to us, must be brought out by our own efforts."

36. ST. ANTHONY BEFORE A CITY. 1519. Engraving

Thereby he wishes "to light a small spark" and spare others a long and difficult road. A well-trained artist does not require a model for every human figure, since he need only pour out what he has amassed over the years: "In such a way will the secret treasure the heart has stored up be revealed through the work and the new creature that a man creates within his own heart in the form of a thing." And then he finds these magnificent words: "A good painter puts himself inside every figure, and if it were possible for him to live forever, from his store of those innate Ideas about which Plato wrote he would over and over again find something new to pour out into his work."

Dürer attacked those who accused art of serving heathenish ends (he meant, of course, the Anabaptists and iconoclasts): "It happens often, because of the interference of the uncouth who would like to stamp out art, that men who possess noble genius are likewise snuffed out." A good Christian is no more likely to be induced into idolatry through paintings and pictures than a pious man into murder by the mere fact that he wears a sword at his side. Indeed, "he must, in truth, be a stupid lout who would pray to a thing of paint or wood." He swears by Luther and flies into a rage over the cult of the Virgin at Regensburg as a gross indecency—and nevertheless in Aachen promptly takes himself off to see "Our Lady's shift."

Dürer's feeling for detail was unique and distinguishes him from all the Italians and French: "It is no good for a painter just to splash something in and try

37. CHRIST ON THE MOUNT OF OLIVES. 1521. Pen drawing. *Städel Institute, Frankfurt am Main*

38. THE APSE OF THE GROOTE KERK IN BERGEN OP ZOOM. 1520. Silverpoint drawing. *Städel Institute, Frankfurt am Main*

to improvise; the tiniest detail should be done skill-fully and as well as possible, nor should the slightest wrinkles and puckers be omitted"; in short, the entire picture should be done with the same alert attention. For this reason he made a distinction between "run-of-the-mill paintings, of which I can dash off a great pile in a year," and others, to which he devoted careful or special effort.

He set up a kind of value judgment, which is intellec-tual not too unlike the single standard of our time. For him, talking about something and actually making it were clearly not the same. "An understanding, ex-perienced artist can better reveal his great power and art in trifling pieces than many others in their largest works. That is why one man can scribble something in pen and ink on a half-sheet of paper in a single day or dig out something from a small block of wood with a little scalpel and it turns out to be more full of art and better than someone else's great work over which he has sweated an entire year." He was perfectly capable of judging differences in quality—as in copperplate

engravings, in which no two prints are ever exactly alike—and his instinct never failed him when it came to knowing what was right for the quite different media of engraving, woodcut, drawing, or painting. "What is too easily dashed off cannot be very rich in art, whereas what is truly artistic demands applica-tion, effort, and hard work. And yet, if we can never attain to the very highest excellence, should we then stop trying to learn? A cowlike notion like that is not for us!"

A few of his ideas do, admittedly, strike us as rather odd. For one, his certainty that only the artist can tell what is good and that, at best, most people can only grasp that something is beautiful. This, surpris-ingly, goes along with his insistence that wholly un-learned commonfolk should be allowed to pass judg-ment because "they are able to recognize if a thing has been done very clumsily, even though they have no way of knowing if it is good." Likewise odd to our times is his notion that beauty results from putting together a great many single parts selected for their

45

BILIBALDI·PIRKEYMHERI·EFFIGIES
AETATIS·SVAE·ANNO·L·III
VIVITVR·INGENIO·CAETERA·MORTIS·
ERVNT·
·M·D·XX·IV·

39. MADONNA AND CHILD. 1520. Engraving   40. WILLIBALD PIRCKHEIMER. 1524. Engraving

41. ST. PHILIP. 1526. Engraving   42. PEASANTS AT MARKET. 1519. Engraving

43. THE LAST SUPPER. 1523. Woodcut

individual beauty, but this is an idea passed on from antiquity, which haunted even a Raphael. We cannot overlook this in Dürer, though he himself justifies it with the poetic fancy of honey made from the sweets of many flowers. Over and over again he is gnawed by anxiety lest he overshoot the right mean, and so tends to sum up his theory in the simple dictum: what is beautiful is that which is without defect.

Dürer the man is revealed to us with all his lovable qualities in the family chronicle, the diaries, and the letters. We know how shaken he was by the grim life of his parents and by their deaths. He was haunted by all sorts of superstitious fears and was not ashamed to

express his anxieties openly. In a dream vision of 1525, set down in watercolor accompanied by a text, there seems to be a prophetic intimation of the atomic explosions of our time (fig. 45).

As a friend, he was full of entertaining caprices, much given to jokes and teasing. In his youth he was something of a dandy, and a handsome new doublet or mantle was good enough news to be noted down for posterity in his diary. He was unassuming, coveted no man's luck, was generous, and drank for more than to quench his thirst. Melanchthon summed him up as "a wise man whose artistic talents, eminent as they were, were still the least of his virtues."

47

44. HEAD OF ST. MARK. 1526. Metalpoint drawing. *State Museums, Berlin-Dahlem*

BIOGRAPHICAL OUTLINE

1471   MAY 21: Albrecht Dürer, son of the goldsmith Albrecht Dürer, born in Nuremberg.

1481–82   Attends the Latin school at the church of St. Lawrence.

1483–86   Studies the goldsmith's craft with his father.

1486–89   Studies painting with Michael Wolgemut.

1490–94   Wanderyears, the later ones along the Upper Rhine.

1494   JULY 7: Marries Agnes Frey in Nuremberg.

1494–95   First visit to Italy.

1498   The Apocalypse and part of the Large Passion.

1504   The Life of Mary series. The *Adam and Eve* engraving.

1505–7   Second visit to Italy.

1509   Acquires the house at the Tiergärtner Gate.

1510–11   Completes the Life of Mary and the Large Passion and publishes the Apocalypse, the Large Passion, the Life of Mary, and the Small Woodcut Passion.

1513   Completes the Engraved Passion. Engraves *Knight, Death, and Devil.*

45. DREAM VISION. 1525. Watercolor. *Kunsthistorisches Museum, Vienna*

1514 Engraves *Melencolia I* and *St. Jerome in His Study*.

1515 Does drawings for the prayer book of Emperor Maximilian I and the *Triumphal Arch*. The Emperor awards him an annuity.

1518 Portrays in drawing the Emperor in Augsburg.

1520–21 Visits the Netherlands.

c. 1525 Completes the books on geometry, fortifications, and proportions.

1526 Paints *The Four Apostles*.

1528 APRIL 6: Dies in Nuremberg.

46. CARDINAL MATTHÄUS LANG VON WELLENBURG. Chalk drawing. *Print Room, Basel*

COLORPLATES

Painted 1490

ALBRECHT DÜRER THE ELDER AT SIXTY-THREE

Panel, 48³/₈ × 35"

Uffizi Gallery, Florence

Dürer was no more than nineteen when he painted this first portrait of his father, then aged sixty-three. It is a genuine portrait, a self-contained and independent picture, and were it not dated it would be scarcely credible that its author could really have been so young and would, in later years, make such extraordinary progress.

The picture still belongs to the late Middle Ages, and in manner is not unlike the portraits being done at the time in Franconia and Swabia. The rosary, which makes a single striking note of cinnabar-red in the picture, is held in rather plump hands which, like those in the drawing of 1486 (W 3), express deep devotion. Basically, the portrait of the elderly man dressed in a woolen cap and fur-lined jacket is much like that of the donor in any religious painting, absorbed in prayer, his gaze directed inward, not outward as in a portrait.

The back of the panel has the double coat of arms of the Dürer and Holper families, and this suggests that it may have been the cover of a coffer painting which, when opened, would have shown both husband and wife. As a matter of fact, there was a portrait of Dürer's mother listed along with it in the 1573–74 inventory of Willibald Imhoff the Elder. Now missing, it was sold in 1633, as we know from Hans Hieronymus Imhoff's private ledger—"but they did not think it Dürer's work." However, it cannot be excluded that the companion piece may have been by another painter, and there are further difficulties. If it was a paired portrait, the coat of arms should have appeared on the back of the wife's portrait. Further, here Dürer's father faces left, but in the portraits of the Tuchers done in 1499 the husband, holding a ring, looks to the right toward his wife. However, there is also the possibility that the companion piece may have been an Ecce Homo or a Madonna.

SELF-PORTRAIT AT TWENTY-TWO

Tempera and oil on vellum, transferred to canvas, $22^{1}/_{4} \times 17^{1}/_{2}$"
The Louvre, Paris

If a few painters before Dürer had actually portrayed themselves, it was usually disguised as one of the figures in an altarpiece. Dürer's youthful self-portrait, however, is the earliest ever painted as an independent picture, or at least the earliest which has come down to us, although he had in fact portrayed himself before, once in a silverpoint drawing done when he was only thirteen (Albertina, fig. 4) and twice in pen and ink during his wanderyears (Erlangen, W 26, and New York, W 27).

The inscription, "My sach die gat / Als es oben schtat," means that his future will be as God has decided.

Abroad at the time, Dürer sent the picture home, probably to be used in the betrothal negotiations, although recent research suggests that it may have been intended solely for his parents.

Dürer is twenty-two here. His nose and lips have become much more prominent since the silverpoint drawing, and the somewhat splayed ear lobe recalls the ink portrait (W 27) and the early *Ecce Homo* (page 57). The young man, whose blond hair is crowned by a red tasseled cap, turns toward the viewer's right. His right forearm—actually his left, since he painted what he saw in a mirror—with the hand holding a sprig of Eryngium (whose name in German means "man's fidelity") rests on an invisible ledge, as does also the rather puffy left hand. Rose-violet ribbons bind the pleated shirt billowing out under the gray mantle and contribute to the great charm of the color in this picture.

The portrait, a copy of which Goethe admired in Helmstedt, was acquired by the Louvre in the First World War by sequestration.

54

ECCE HOMO

Panel, 11¹³/₁₆ × 7¹/₂"

Staatliche Kunsthalle, Karlsruhe

Previously unknown, this small devotional painting, whose embossed gold background must once have been mostly covered by a Gothic frame, turned up in Karlsruhe in 1941. Because of the war, several years went by before Dürer specialists gave it their almost universal consensus, and today it is quite certain that it is an authentic work by Dürer.

It may well have been done during the artist's wanderyears, most likely in 1494. With Martin Schongauer's engraving *The Man of Sorrows* (B 69) it has in common the pointed arch of the background and the close-up foreground ledge behind which Christ sits as if within a kind of grotto. The head leans heavily on the right arm, which in turn rests on the knee of the upraised right leg to create a richly plastic movement in highly expressive contrast with the quiet gaze of Christ which fixes the viewer. The underlying mood is much like that of the title page of the Small Woodcut Passion.

Especially significant for the attribution of the picture are the analogies with the fingers in others of Dürer's works. Those of the right hand are fine-boned, as is usual with Dürer, and the rather ugly thumb of the left hand is identical with that in the *Self-Portrait* of 1493 (page 55).

56

THE DEATH OF ST. DOMINIC

Panel, $37^3/_8 \times 30^3/_4''$

Landesmuseum, Darmstadt

In the Darmstadt museum there are several large fragments of an altarpiece dedicated to St. Dominic, and a smaller section is in the Munich Alte Pinakothek. Not until relatively late did scholars turn their attention to it. For us today it is difficult to imagine how the entire altarpiece looked originally, but it can be conjectured that the *Lamentation* and *Flagellation*, both of which have been cut at the sides, and the *Taking of Christ*, which has been shortened both above and below, were all initially of the same dimensions and made up the outer wings of a triptych which, opened, revealed the Death, Ascension, and Coronation of St. Dominic. Nevertheless, it cannot be ruled out that the fragments may have come from two separate altarpieces.

It is generally agreed that the young Dürer was taken on as a journeyman by some Strassburg master whom he assisted mostly on altarpieces. For this polyptych, one can be quite sure that Dürer himself painted at least the Ascension and Coronation and, especially, the Death of the Saint. When it is realized that the work must have been completed no later than 1494, there is reason to marvel at how few medieval Late Gothic traits it has, how modern in conception it was for the time.

One has the impression that the Saint was suddenly overcome by weakness, that a mattress of plaited rushes was quickly pushed under him, and he was laid on the stairs leading into a room while the tiny female donor with banderoles was called in to aid at the tragic event. St. Dominic is no wasted ascetic but, even on his deathbed, a man firmly planted in life. He still has enough strength to take hold of the candle given him by one of the four brethren who busy themselves about him. Another of the monks sprinkles holy water over the dying man while a third folds his hands in prayer and is himself consoled by a fourth monk. The brethren in the background pray, and one leafs through a book. To one side there is the partial figure of a hooded old woman.

Once again we are struck by the importance given to hands. The Saint presses his index and middle fingers together and separates the other two fingers in such characteristic fashion that it can be considered a further development of the finger position in the *Self-Portrait* of 1493. An analogous disposition of the fingers is found in a sketch sheet in the Albertina (W 47).

The conception and treatment of wrinkled flesh in the right hand of the monk who joins his hands in prayer is so fine that we are irresistibly reminded of the hand of the sorrowing Mother of God in the Passion altarpiece of the Munich Alte Pinakothek.

POND IN THE WOODS

Watercolor and gouache, $10^{5}/_{16} \times 14^{3}/_{4}''$
British Museum, London

This watercolor is closely related to the *House on an Island in a Pond* which was used as a study for the copperplate engraving *The Madonna with the Monkey* (B 42) dated around 1498. For this reason, to date the two watercolors at the same time as the engraving, as has been done, is simply not acceptable. Since it is based on the watercolor, the engraving must be of a later date, and since perspective in the engraving is handled with greater precision, it must be presumed that some time elapsed between the execution of the watercolor and of the engraving. What is most likely is that the two watercolors date from shortly before the first trip to Italy, that is mid-1494.

This watercolor differs from those done during the sojourn in Italy. The latter adhere to certain definite prototypes, whereas here there is a freedom and originality of conception scarcely found before except in Leonardo da Vinci. Most astonishing is the way the blue pool stretches toward the horizon, open and infinite as the sea. In contrast, the tufts of grass in the foreground are rendered with utmost accuracy. If Dürer started out with a more painstaking and precise conception in mind, we have no need to lament that he did not go through with it. What he achieved is, in fact, a vision of primeval nature. The wood to the right is made up of spruce trees which seem to move as if alive and yet stand their ground however insecurely they may be rooted. But to the left are dead trunks, symbols of despair like those we have come to know in the great wars of our time. Linked as they are to the heavy-hanging dark-blue streaks of cloud, the impression they create is of an apocalyptic waste and void which freezes us with its menace.

60

WEHLSCH PIRG (ITALIAN MOUNTAIN)

Watercolor and gouache, $8^1/_4 \times 12^5/_{16}$"
Ashmolean Museum, Oxford

Among the watercolors done on the first journey to Italy, the *Wehlsch pirg* (W 99) —Dürer's own inimitable German locution for "Italian mountain"—stands out as the most like a very quick sketch. Generally in the watercolors of that period Dürer recorded every detail he saw, but here he did it only for the centermost mountain with its ridge stretching away to the left. There he shows how some areas are covered with thick forest, others with scrub, isolated trees, or bare trunks. It is as if the artist had trained field glasses on the mountain and, satisfied with what he found there, left all the rest unfocused.

The special fascination of this picture lies precisely in the way he used broad brush strokes and flowing washes to give an impression of the foothills on the right with their lesser humps and indented valleys, and then echoed this in the high mountain behind them. Only a church halfway up the loosely brushed-in slope is more meticulously delineated.

Fascinating too is the way that beyond the faint blue-green ridge the view takes in the milky brownish-white distance against which lie a bluish-violet stretch of mountain and an even more remote peak and, trailing above them, strands of cloud drawn in with the fine brush Dürer favored at the time. The soft tones together with the pale tan foreground set the time as early morning. All of this is not unrelated to the distant view of mountains in *St. Jerome in the Wilderness* (page 67).

Naturally, scholars have tried to pin down the exact site Dürer painted, and most convincing is the suggestion of A. Rusconi that it is the Val di Cembra in the locality of Segonzano near what is today Mezzocorona.

ARCO

Watercolor and gouache, $8\,^{11}/_{16} \times 8\,^{11}/_{16}''$
The Louvre, Paris

Arco (W 94) is one of the most painstakingly worked-out watercolors Dürer did on his first trip to Italy. Such patience can only be ascribed to the excitement of first discovery, and this means that it must have been done on the outward journey to Italy, during a side trip from Trent to Lake Garda.

The mountain is crowned by a fortified tower surrounded by a crenelated wall. Even the steep wooded slope is studded with towers and a defensive wall which is capped by houses and crenelated towers as far as the middle row of fortifications. The mountain road climbing to the summit is guarded by round towers and notched battlements which also watch over the town and church at the foot of the mountain. The foreground is made up of fertile olive groves and vineyards, and the entire view is framed by a precipitous cliff face on the left and a ridge in the foreground, where the painter must have sat to record this scene.

The viewer's delight surely lies in the previously unheard-of finely detailed treatment of walls, battlements, roofs, and windows. Despite the spaciousness of the scene, Dürer avoided all effects of steep perspective. Thus he created a unified tonal quality, thereby tying together the grayish fields and battlements, the brownish roofs, the light green of the olive trees. No one can doubt that this is by the same hand that engraved the landscape in the *Nemesis*, which was based on a similar watercolor now lost.

ST. JEROME IN THE WILDERNESS

Panel, 9 $^1/_{16}$ × 6 $^{13}/_{16}$″

Collection Lt. Col. Sir Edmund Bacon, Raveningham Hall, Norwich

It was only in 1957 that this miniature-like panel was discovered in the attic of an English country house.

The bearded bald Father of the Church kneels in a loose-hanging overshirt-like blue garment in a richly detailed brown-and-green landscape of rocky foothills sweeping away to distant peaks. At the horizon, clouds streak the yellowish sky of early morning. The Saint holds in his left hand a stone with which he beats his breast, in his right a red book which serves to create an impression of spatial depth. His cardinal's mantle and hat, similar patches of red, are scattered before him on a swath of grass thickly overgrown with forest plants and flowers (which can be identified) and enlivened by a bullfinch, a goldfinch, and a butterfly (as in the *Holy Family* engraving, B 44, but not, as Panofsky notes, the kind of butterfly Germans call "God's Worshiper").

What we have here is a concentrated cosmos in which man too has an organic part. It was St. Jerome, in one of his letters, who said that "we marvel at the Creator not only in the heavens and the earth, in the sun and great seas, in elephants, camels, horses, sheep, leopards, bears, lions, but also in the tiniest creatures—ants, midges, worms, and suchlike minute beasts whose appearances are more familiar to us than their names." Such ideas can be found also in Alberti's writings. It is quite possible that the back of the panel, which is painted with an apocalyptic planetary vision with extraordinary clouds and a gigantic asymmetrically radiating star, likewise has to do with St. Jerome, to whom, as is known, was vouchsafed a revelation of the destruction of the world.

Behind St. Jerome, to the left, lies the lion which always accompanied the Saint after he had delivered it of a thorn in its paw. The lion constitutes an apparently valid basis for dating the picture, since it closely resembles that in the miniature (W 65) in the Hamburg Kunsthalle dated 1494. It seems that at that time Dürer, who was of course familiar with the conventional heraldic type, took the opportunity of sketching from life the lions he saw in a cage in Venice.

The wooded rocks recall those in the engraved *St. Jerome* (B 61) and are based on a study of a quarry (W 108) done around 1496, after Dürer's return from Italy. According to information supplied me by Professor Martini of the State Institute for Soil Study in Hanover, such virtually perpendicular strata are not a figment of Dürer's imagination but can be found in the district of Brenta and in the Tauern massif near Sterzing.

It seems safe to conclude that this small panel, like the *St. Christopher* in Dessau, must have been done on the trip to Venice.

ELECTOR FREDERICK THE WISE OF SAXONY

Tempera on canvas, 29⁷/₈ × 22¹/₂″

State Museums, Berlin-Dahlem

Most of Dürer's paintings in tempera on canvas are in poor condition now. This portrait is one of the best preserved, although even here time has taken its toll: one eye is overly sunken into the darkness of its socket, the black headgear was formerly more detailed.

Here we have the prince who later championed Luther and had the brilliant idea of taking him into "protective custody" on the Wartburg, thereby demonstrating a virtue all too rare in Germanic countries throughout history, namely, civil courage. Although in three-quarter profile turned toward the right, he looks directly at the viewer so that his dark-brown right eye becomes a fixed point in the composition and, at the same time, fixes on itself the viewer's attention. Rather unlike the more good-humored copperplate-engraved portrait of 1524, here there is something reserved, a little posed about the man. He wants us to see him as a master among men who holds his counsel but bores into the heart of every question with his quiet, all-controlling eyes. Early on, this man with the long sharp nose and full lower lip had a keen perception of the worth of art and artists and became Dürer's special patron. It is significant that the Elector should have commissioned various altarpieces from a twenty-five-year-old artist and should afterward never wholly have lost sight of him.

Frederick is dressed in a black doublet, and his slashed sleeves are encircled by ornamental gold galloons. Over the doublet he wears a lightweight black capelet which is trimmed in the same fashion and leaves his right shoulder and arm exposed. His hands are crossed; the left one holds a small scroll of writing and rests on a ledge which, as in so many pictures of the time, is used to give the impression of depth. The gaping doublet lets us catch a glimpse of a shirt of gold brocade patterned with blue and red blossoms and green foliage. The gray-green background contrasts with the lifelike ruddy complexion of the hands and the face framed by beard and moustache and rather curly hair.

THE ALTARPIECE OF THE MADONNA

Tempera on canvas. Central picture 37³/₈ × 41¹/₂″, wings 44¹/₈ × 17¹/₈″
Staatliche Gemäldegalerie, Dresden

Dürer could have learned equally well from either Schongauer or the Italians the device of a foreground ledge to define and deepen the pictorial space. Here, in the central picture, which is somewhat cut down at the top, it serves also to give prominence to the Child asleep on it. Mary turns from her open prayer book, likewise resting on the ledge, to bow, hands joined, in adoration before her Son. She herself stands behind the ledge, framed by the rigorously vertical walls.

The background is made up of an almost empty room with two glimpses of scenes outside it. Through the window one sees an open place with many-storied buildings which, apparently, no one has as yet identified. The door opens onto a carpenter shop where Joseph goes about his tasks. Everywhere tiny angels busy themselves, some sweeping the floor, others soaring above the Madonna, among whom two hold a crown above her.

The painting belongs to a moderately large altarpiece with two side panels. On the left is the bearded St. Anthony, his right hand resting on his left which holds upright on the ledge an open book in such a way that it echoes both the vertical and horizontal lines of the picture. Above the Saint rages war between tiny angels and devils, evil spirits, and demons. One of the angels makes ready the circlet destined for the Saint's crown.

On the right side panel is the powerful half-length nude of St. Sebastian with hands joined in prayer. In front of him, on the ledge, are placed a glass with a sprig of quaking grass, a piece of bread, and half of an apple. The Saint appears as an ascetic, young in years but old in suffering, and above him too soar angels holding aloft not only the instruments of his martyrdom but also his promised crown.

Out of these childlike angels who wage war or exult over victory Dürer created something richly meaningful which accounts for a good deal of the charm of this altarpiece: a kind of angelic concert not dissimilar, in terms of pictorial function, to the golden arabesques adorning the upper parts of Gothic carved altars.

The altarpiece was commissioned in 1496 by the Elector Frederick and remained until 1687 in the castle chapel at Wittenberg.

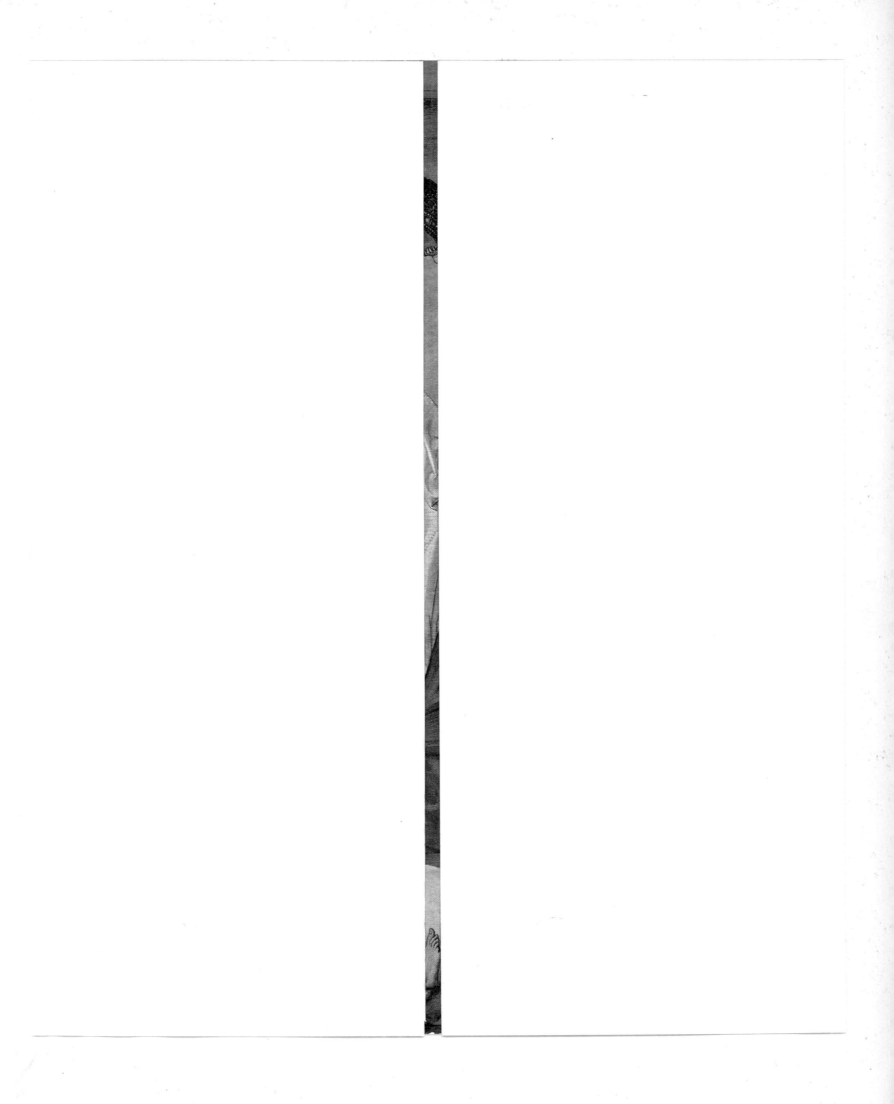

Painted 1497

ALBRECHT DÜRER THE ELDER
AT SEVENTY

Panel, 20 $^1/_8 \times 16^1/_8$ "

The National Gallery, London

For too long this picture has not been appreciated as it should be, probably because the background and inscription have been repainted to such an extent as to disturb the harmony of the whole, although the face itself is in excellent condition. It was generally thought to be a copy, but in recent years there is more and more agreement that it is not only the original but also of outstanding quality.

Dürer's father is portrayed here as an almost frontal three-quarter-length figure. He wears a cap fitting close to the ears, his mantle hangs in loose folds like a judge's gown, and its wide sleeves are held overlapping so that one can make out no more than a few fingers, the permanently dirt-grimed fingers of a craftsman. Compared with the portrait from 1490 (page 53), the man has aged more than the few years' difference would lead us to expect. The burdens once cheerfully assumed now weigh heavily on a stronger, more stubborn, more self-confident man. One senses that his life could not have been easy, and this we know from his son's family chronicle: "Item, the afore-mentioned Albrecht Dürer passed his earthly days in great effort and grinding hard work. He knew many discouragements, disputes, and calamities, and was a man of few words."

The face has aged much. The thin lips are tightly sealed with something of bitterness, the nose is thickened and bulkier, and where, earlier, the eyes with their fixed expression of piety were brightened by a glimmer of light, here they reveal no more than cautious reserve and a sharply critical outlook on life. And yet, this is the same man who, five years before, in a letter to his wife from Linz could recount with evident satisfaction that the Emperor Frederick III himself had tendered him the payment for his work and said to him, "My goldsmith, now betake yourself to the inn and do yourself proud."

LOT AND HIS DAUGHTERS

Panel, 19³/₄ × 15⁵/₈"

National Gallery of Art, Washington, D.C. (Kress Collection)

This scene is on the back of the panel of the so-called *Haller Madonna*, a painting whose attractiveness lies in large measure in its excellent state of preservation. There the Child, upright on a cushion, is a not very handsome, fattish, and not exactly young boy from whom one could expect almost anything except that later he might pronounce the Sermon on the Mount. The Virgin is much like the Magdalene in the Glimm *Lamentation over the Dead Christ* of 1500, although there one can justify the mantle shrouding the head as an attempt to create an effect of monumentality.

The back of the panel, with Lot and his daughters treated in a happy tongue-in-cheek manner, is, therefore, so much the more delightful. The bearded old man trots doggedly forward, his wine flask slung over his shoulder. His cloak is lined with lamb's wool, and his striding movement lets us glimpse his legs and part of his tunic. In his left hand he carries a basket full of eggs, and on his head he sports a yellow turban jammed down under some kind of red-and-green winged headgear. One daughter is dressed in bright vermilion and daintily lifts her skirt with her right hand to let us see her blue-green undergarment, while her left hand steadies a large bundle carried peasant-fashion on her head. Her somewhat smaller younger sister in a brownish garment carries the family moneybox and, in her left hand, yarn and a distaff. Everything then is shipshape, and the pair of them, as Buchner remarked, look the picture of innocence. Their mother, though, has already paid for her mistake: she looked back and was turned into a pillar of salt some distance behind in the great rock pass which opens up toward the right, where we can see Sodom and Gomorrah consumed in clouds of brimstone and fire which tower to the heavens: "And, lo, the smoke of the country went up as the smoke of a furnace." This world we know already: it is the world of the Apocalypse series.

THE PAUMGARTNER ALTARPIECE
(central panel, detail)

Panel, 61 × 49³/₈"

Alte Pinakothek, Munich

This altarpiece (see fig. 11) takes its name from the Paumgartner family who, in *The Nativity* of the central panel, are portrayed very small as the donors: the father, two sons, and a fourth person on the left, the mother and two daughters, one married, the other single, on the right. On the side panels there are large figures of the son Stefan portrayed as St. George on the left, and the other son Lucas as St. Eustace on the right, both set against solid black backgrounds. These identifications are traditional and may well be the other way around.

The central panel exploits the same boxlike space as the Dresden altarpiece (page 71) except that here, in place of the window ledge and walls, a farmyard stretches out, hemmed in by walls and buildings, to create a stage on which the figures play their parts. Beneath a flimsy overhanging porch the Madonna bows in adoration before her Child. Outside the porch, the fragile elderly Joseph in white and wine-red mantle kneels with his lantern (it is night), with an awkward grace. Neither he nor Mary with her bluish-white headkerchief actually looks at the Christ Child held up on a fold of Mary's capacious dark-blue mantle by a swarm of little angels who themselves weave an enchanting garland of figures completed on either side by the tiny donors. In an architectural setting of ruins—to the right Romanesque columns behind which an ox and an ass look out, to the left three-dimensional stone blocks and arches in which appear two shepherds— everything conspires to emphasize the effect of perspective, which is further stressed by the planks laid across the great stone arch in the background through whose vast round opening we see, soaring aloft, the tiny Angel of the Annunciation. From the background approach two shepherds clearly differentiated in manner and movement. This, from the standpoint of painting, is the most progres-

(continued on page 78)

THE PAUMGARTNER ALTARPIECE
(right wing, St. Eustace)

Panel, 61³/₄×24"

Alte Pinakothek, Munich

(continued from page 76)
sive element in the entire picture. The reddish overgarment of the shepherd to
the right and the light-blue collar of the one to the left create a kind of crisscross
echo to the colors of the principal figures in the foreground. As for the light
source at the upper left, it is a matter of preference whether it should be called a
midnight sun, a miraculous *sol novus*, or more simply a gigantic corona-encircled
full moon.

The idea of filling the two wings with full-length portraits of the donor's sons
was something completely unheard of. Furthermore, the distribution of their
weight between fixed and free legs was an innovation impossible without the
lessons Dürer had learned in Italy. One young man stands massively, his gaze
directed toward the right, his left hand idly patting the vanquished dragon at his
side. His brother (opposite page) is slenderer, more wiry, in many respects still
Gothic. Over their armor each wears a distinctive slashed leather jacket, vermilion
or wine-red, and George has red stockings, Eustace red tights and knee-high
leather boots. Each holds a fluttering white banner as a clue to his identity: the
red cross of St. George, the stag's head of St. Eustace with the crucifix between
its antlers.

A seventeenth-century manuscript description of the Imperial city of Nuremberg, now in the Germanic Museum there, records that in the year 1498 Albrecht
Dürer portrayed Stefan and Lucas Paumgartner as St. George and St. Eustace on
an altarpiece for the cloister church of St. Catherine. This suffices to date the
painting, and yet, although the stylistic traits are in complete accord with that
date, there are still some doubters who cannot believe such a painting could have
been done before 1500.

78

THE LAMENTATION
OVER THE DEAD CHRIST (detail)

Panel, 59 1/2 × 47 5/8"

Alte Pinakothek, Munich

Of the two Lamentations, that for the Holzschuher family in Nuremberg and the present one, done for the Glimms and now in Munich, the latter must be later in date. It was commissioned for the Dominican church in Nuremberg by the family of the goldsmith Albrecht Glimm, and they are portrayed as tiny kneeling figures at the lower edge of the picture.

The way the right hand of the dead Christ is lifted away from the corpse by one of the Marys (who is dressed in material which shimmers between red and yellow and green) was at the time a new motif devised to enhance the feeling of space. The central group forms a triangle with as apex the Madonna with her bluish-white headkerchief, while the other figures form another much larger triangle whose sides roughly parallel and enclose that of the main group. On the left, Nicodemus supports the dead Christ under the arms, on the right Joseph of Arimathea stands clutching an end of the linen winding sheet in one hand while holding an urn in the other. The triangular mound of figures culminates in the St. John strikingly garbed in yellow, reddish violet, and gray. Whatever might smack too strongly of self-conscious constructivism in the composition is minimized by the interposition in the center right of the figure of Mary Magdalene with her vermilion mantle drawn over her head and her vase of oil held in both hands; a similar interruption of the geometrical structure is provided by another woman, center left, with hands upraised in wild gesticulation, a motif familiar from Netherlandish and Italian art.

The diagonally laid-out blue-and-green mountainous background is articulated by a hill town halfway up, once again a recollection from the first trip to Italy, and together mountain and town form another pair of triangles, one enclosed in the other. In short, the composition may be reduced to geometrical forms, which are saved from becoming obvious by the many individual details.

A tree on the left and the center post of the Cross toward the right introduce markedly vertical elements, while a gigantic black storm cloud not only leaves the mountains gleaming and, through the effect of light, draws them forward into the picture but also streaks the tragic foreground with doleful shadow.

SELF-PORTRAIT AT TWENTY-NINE

Panel, 26³/₈ × 19¹/₄"

Alte Pinakothek, Munich

The admirers of this third self-portrait were—and still are—tempted to ascribe the achievement to Italy, to take it as an exemplary prototype of the Renaissance spirit. But neither Italy nor the Renaissance fully accounts for it. In all of Italian art there is nothing like it: Italian art lacks this profound ethical spirit, the unflinching earnestness which pervades every detail of this portrait and is most deeply expressed in the transfixing eyes. As for the Renaissance, here there is a question of symmetry: the axis is clearly displaced toward the left, and not merely to allow room for the inscription. The fact is, the painting has much less of the spirit of the Italian Renaissance, always more attuned to what is both harmonious and worldly, than of the age which preceded it. Despite all its modern aspects, it is best explained in terms of medieval piety. It is the Dürer of the Apocalypse— not the Dürer of the Life of Mary or *The Madonna of the Rose Garlands*—who puts the question here: "Who am I?" It is the Dürer who has taken upon himself the mission of holding up a mirror to the anxieties of mankind. This he had already done in the Apocalypse, but here he turns the mirror on himself as one of God's creatures. Beauty for Dürer was something divine. If the portrait is constructed like an icon—a German scheme rather than Italian, as Kehrer pointed out—it is because in itself proportion, the measured mean, contains for Dürer something of divinity. The human figure here in its spiritual beauty becomes a kind of deep enigma, and in that it is worlds apart from the equally significant self-portrait of 1498 (frontispiece), which is far more mundane, though even it is not wholly so.

The resemblance to Christ, who was always depicted with hair parted boldly in the middle, is neutralized by an off-center single lock across the forehead, and with luxuriant wavy hair flowing down to the shoulders. This may disturb present-day viewers of the portrait, but the picture is unthinkable apart from these deliberately stimulated associations. The fascination is enhanced by the contemporary and quite worldly clothing: a brown fur-lined mantle with slashed sleeves whose satiny insets seem grayish in contrast to the tiny triangle of immaculate white shirt visible where the fur lapels cross. The broadly laid-on flesh tints, delicate as they are, stand out strikingly and yet remain in key with the underlying tone of the entire picture.

Of formal significance is the asymmetrically placed right hand (the painter's left, of course, since he is seeing himself in a mirror), but it is also an image of the greatest sensitivity: in his 1532 translation of Dürer's book *Human Proportions*, Camerarius comments, "*Sed digitis nihil dixisses vidisse elegantius*"—"never will you behold anything more elegant than those fingers."

Although the data given are correct, the inscription is not authentic. Originally it was written out on a small curved shield which was covered over when the background, probably initially brightly colored, was painted over dark.

Painted 1500

PORTRAIT OF A YOUNG MAN

Panel, $11 \times 8^{1}/_{4}''$

Alte Pinakothek, Munich

This portrait, rather questionably claimed by some to be of one of Dürer's brothers, is one of the best-painted pictures of the early period, if not the best, along
with the self-portrait of the same year which hangs on the same wall in Munich.
Like the latter, it is painted with attention to tonal values and to surface qualities.

Dürer's work from that period must be distinguished not merely on the basis he
himself used—according to the effort and time put in—but also on the grounds
of the format employed. In the Paumgartner altarpiece, for example, the head of
the young Lucas as St. Eustace is handled with emphasis on line and drawing,
and this is typical of the large-scale works of Dürer's early period. But in small
works, as here, the artist allowed full play to his painterly intuition. The tradition
he carried on in his portraits had been developing for decades in Nuremberg, and
much of worth had been achieved by his teacher Wolgemut as well as by Pleydenwurff and many artists whose names have been lost to us.

This energetic, bony, badly shaved face could belong to any of the apprentices
in Wolgemut's workshop, from whom, as Dürer himself recounts, he had to
endure much annoyance—indeed, it has something in common with the tormentors of Christ so frequently depicted at the time. The cold eyes under the prominent
dark-brown eyebrows are gray, the complexion tannish to tannish red in the
cheeks, the mouth with its protruding lower lip rather asymmetrical, the ear
rendered in all its details.

The young man is dressed in a blackish-brown jerkin or shirt under a tobacco-
brown smock, though not much can be made out of either. His brown headgear,
folded in rings and jammed down over his head, juts out over a dark skullcap
which is the color of his jerkin, and it is foreshortened in a way to bring out more
prominently the line of the cheek. Even if the picture were not already dated by
the artist, the headgear would suffice to date this timeless portrait.

Painted 1502

THE HARE

Watercolor and gouache, $9^7/_8 \times 8^7/_8''$
Albertina, Vienna

In the years after 1500 Dürer turned his attention to everything the eye can per-
ceive in life and, in particular, to every creature "that creepeth and flieth." Indeed,
the objectively visible became, for the first time, the chief concern of his art.
Evidence of this is *The Madonna with Many Animals* (which has survived in three
versions using drawing or watercolor, all dated 1503) and the introduction of all
sorts of beasts into the *Adam and Eve* engraving (fig. 12) where the garden is
enlivened with a cat, a mouse, an elk, an ox, a parakeet, and—a hare. For the latter
he made quick pen sketches (W 359), although frolicking hares had appeared as
early as the large woodcut *Holy Family with Three Hares* (B 102) and were to
appear again later, in 1509, in the *Holy Family in the Hall* (W 466, in Basel), not
that one can always distinguish between "hares" and "rabbits."

This *Hare* (W 248) is something quite different. It is *the* hare, the hare pure and
simple, the Platonic Idea of the hare. Whatever Dürer's familiarity may have been
with Plato's visionary conception—and his writings show that he was acquainted
with it—this would have meant very little were he not a gifted painter capable of
visualizing for himself what for the Greek was a purely philosophical abstraction.
The master himself knew this, and that is why he signed and dated the watercolor
with such care, as if to make it clear beyond doubt that here he had done something
special.

Dürer chose the position most characteristic of the animal: crouched on a
diagonal from left to right, the forepaws close together and firmly gripping the
ground, the long ears waving and well distinguished one from the other, the fur
sleek and soft, its underparts less smoothly brushed and a little dampish. First the
artist laid down an underpainting in watercolor shading from light brown to
gray, then with a fine-pointed brush he drew in the individual hairs and fuzz of
the fur and the white highlights and dark whiskers, all of this with such care that
even the fur of the body and that of the ears are clearly differentiated. In such a
feat, no painter afterward ever surpassed Dürer.

SALVATOR MUNDI

Panel, 22¹/₂ × 18¹/₂"

The Metropolitan Museum of Art, New York (Michael Friedsam Collection)

Dürer never finished this painting of Christ as the Saviour of the World, a half-length figure with the right hand raised in benediction over the terrestrial globe held in the left. There is much reason to believe that it was begun before the second journey to Italy, that is, before the autumn of 1505. It was intended for the central panel of a small altarpiece whose wings, likewise unfinished, depicted John the Baptist and St. Onophrius. These were in the Bremen Kunsthalle where, during the last war, the panel with the Baptist was tragically lost.

The picture is of special interest because of the fascination always attached to what is unfinished. It constitutes the proof that, right from the start of his conceptions, Dürer thought fundamentally as a painter. Face, beard, hands, drapery were all carefully sketched in, but then the artist let himself go in a furioso of color, storming about in incandescent fire-red, marvelous sky-blue, carmine, green, which were splashed in with a heavily loaded brush. Only after this basic step did he give thought to shaping his forms more precisely with a finer brush. The picture gives the lie to all those who persist in pigeonholing Dürer as a draftsman and not a painter.

Not without reason it has been said that there is much in this painting which recalls Jacopo de' Barbari, who settled in Nuremberg in 1500 and who himself had come under the influence of Bellini.

Painted 1503

THE GREAT CLUMP OF TURF

Watercolor and gouache, $16^1/_8 \times 12^1/_2$"

Albertina, Vienna

In the same way as Dürer's *Hare* can be considered *the* hare, the true Idea, so this study of grass (W 346) is the quintessential image of grass. It is called "great" merely because there is also a *Small Clump of Turf* (W 357), but even if there were not, this extraordinary picture—executed with no more than gouache and water-color, and with its date of 1503 hidden away in the lower right—would deserve such an epithet.

Unique in its play of shadowy tones of green and gray (painted on a sunless day), unsurpassed in its observation and faithful recording of countless tiny natural-istic details, it is "great" as a supreme example of how a genius views what, to all appearances, is no more than a casual fragment of nature. In his vision, it becomes a world in itself, a microcosm which broadens to take in the macrocosm and is felt as such.

True, one can pick out details: meadow grass, dandelion and ribwort buds, half-hidden in the dark of a broad-leaved plant a wild orchid a botanist could probably name. And yet what remains with one is the impression of the whole as a virtually inextricable clump of vegetation. Nothing is there for itself but only as a detail in relationship with other details. The broad-leaved forms of the leaves of a large ribwort and of a smaller plant behind it are there to create a feeling of depth. The yarrow with its small, finely divided, double-feathered foliage serves as a measure of the other plants towering above it. The steep slope of the patch of earth leads the eye down by gradual stages to the grasses in the foreground with their exposed roots drinking in the watery soil. These parts of the picture contrast with the crisscross stems of the plants lying somewhat farther back in the left half of the picture, out of which rises, tall, a slender blade of double-panicle grass entangled with many other grasses. In numerous other details one can, if one wishes, discern parallels which lead the eye now perpendicularly, now to the right, now to the left (a broken stem, a blade running off in contradiction to the general movement), and all of this brings us to realize that the compositional mastery of the man who created this tangle was such as to encompass even the seeming chaos which many may be inclined to see in this superb picture.

Painted 1504

THE THREE KINGS ALTARPIECE
(The Adoration of the Magi)

Panel, 38⁵/₈ × 44¹/₈"

Uffizi Gallery, Florence

Almost more than in any of his other pictures, *The Adoration of the Magi* brims over with Dürer's love of life. Originally it was the central panel of the polyptych the Elector Frederick the Wise donated to the Wittenberg castle chapel, but today the wings are dispersed in Munich (page 95), Frankfurt, and Cologne (page 97) and, as we know from a drawing in Berlin, there was a predella with *The Banquet of Job's Children*, now lost.

Dürer had treated this subject before, notably in the woodcut Life of Mary series where it is presented as a crowded scene compressed into a narrow space. In this oblong format, however, he aimed at something quite different. Here he could show what is meant by laying out a picture clearly, and, in fact, Wölfflin did not hesitate to term it the first fully and clearly organized picture in all of German art.

First of all, he chose not to place the Madonna in her conventional position in the center. Instead she occupies the lower left area of the picture, and the positions of all the other personages follow logically from this. Even Dürer's great predecessors Stefan Lochner and Rogier van der Weyden had not done a finer rendering of the hands and facial expression of the kneeling King, nor had anyone before dared to portray the Child as a playful infant, leaning forward eagerly to grasp at the golden casket. Behind this group rises the tall figure of the second richly adorned King. He holds a great golden Gothic lidded chalice and looks over toward the Moorish King who has not yet set foot on the stone step leading up to the Child but stands frontally, almost isolated, a beautifully balanced figure (in a pose much like that of Stefan Paumgartner), holding in his gloved right hand a spherical gold vessel, his feathered hat in his left. Only Joseph is absent from the scene, relegated to the left wing now in Munich.

The stone platform and the roofed stall over the ox and ass constitute important factors in creating perspective. In the bright middle ground, parallel or vertical to the plane of the picture, there are ruined arches which, by means of foreshortening or diminishing proportions, increase the impression of spatial depth and, at the same time, serve to make the figures more prominent. In the far distance rises a fortified hill town like those Dürer saw on his first travels in Italy.

THE THREE KINGS ALTARPIECE
(left wing, Joseph and Joachim)

Panel, 37³/₄ × 21¹/₄"

Alte Pinakothek, Munich

We know that after the turn of the century Dürer overcame his obsession with the apocalyptic. Delight in color took the place of what before had been, usually, muted tones. The wings of this altarpiece (once rectangular, according to the Berlin drawing) reveal striking parallels with many details in the Life of Mary woodcuts and are a kind of prelude to the late painting *The Four Apostles*. The two men of God are highly differentiated but have in common their solemn dignity. This is brought out by their splendid red garments strikingly juxtaposed to grassy green or shimmering gold as well as by the gold background which, by that time, represented a return to a past tradition and which, in any case, has been modified from the original.

Joseph is seen in profile looking toward the right, supporting himself on a staff on whose pommel can be made out the artist's signature. In his right hand he holds a gray pilgrim's hat, and over his robe shading from wine-red to vermilion falls a softly draped grass-green tunic of rich material. Joachim, facing him, wears a gold tunic over his wine-red garment and a rose-colored cap trimmed with whitish-gray fur which blends with his whitish-gray beard.

The right-hand wing with Simeon and Lazarus is equally fine. Simeon, his hands folded, wears a dark-red cap and is swathed in a vermilion mantle trimmed with fitch fur. Lazarus is presented as a bishop with golden miter and crosier, dressed in white with a green-lined gold cope.

94

THE THREE KINGS ALTARPIECE
(exterior of right wing, Drummer and Piper)

Panel, 36⁵/₈ × 20¹/₈″

Wallraf-Richartz Museum, Cologne

The familiar depiction of the Mocking of Job actually has no basis in the Bible. At most one can read there how his wife demanded to know if he could still maintain his faith in God despite the fact that Satan had smitten him "with sore boils from the sole of his foot unto his crown," and indeed she counseled him to "curse God, and die."

But that she emptied a bucket of slops over his head is pure invention—though, to tell the truth, she probably could not have found a better means of making her opinion clear. At any rate, that is the way Dürer painted the story on the exterior of the left wing of the altarpiece, which is now in the Staedel Institute, Frankfurt.

Following this, Job's three friends came "to mourn with him and to comfort him," among them Eliphaz the Temanite who debated with the sufferer the problem of why the innocent should be punished, and Job gave him answer. But still there is no mention of the musicians we see here. And whether the pair of them came to mock or to console, they do make a rollicking team, one drumming, the other piping (and the drummer may be another self-portrait).

Although the exterior panels would seem to call for less painstaking execution, the composition, which extends across both wings, is in fact very carefully thought out. Certainly they must have been dashed off more rapidly, but the result is real painterly verve. In any case, there can be no doubt as to their authenticity.

The light-red cape of the drummer contrasts sharply with the green doublet the piper wears over his blouse. The latter's tights are light leather-colored, those of his partner grayish brown. Even their positions echo these contrasts: the piper is seen from the back as he pivots around dragging his right leg behind the left, while the drummer faces forward, solidly planted on a knoll below which one can make out a scene with tiny figures. What is the significance of those figures? Here at last the Biblical text is of help. In the first chapter of the Book of Job, we read how Satan, after winning the Lord's consent, wreaked his fury on Job's possessions. While Job's children were happily feasting, there came a messenger to recount how the enemy swooped down, fell upon the oxen and asses, "and took them away; yea, they have slain the servants with the edge of the sword; and I only am escaped alone to tell thee."

Dürer did not always work as freely and happily as here, and so perhaps something cheerful emerges from these panels that seems to have little to do with their far from happy subject.

Painted 1505

PORTRAIT OF A VENETIAN WOMAN

Panel, $13^3/_4 \times 10^1/_4''$

Kunsthistorisches Museum, Vienna

It was a great surprise to everyone in 1923 when this dated and signed portrait turned up in a Lithuanian private collection, from which the Vienna museum was able to acquire it. There could be no doubt that it was from Dürer's own hand, not alone because of the signature but also because the picture accorded perfectly with generally accepted notions of how Dürer painted during his second Italian sojourn as evidenced by *The Madonna of the Rose Garlands* plus a good many portraits of men and one of a woman. While the latter was provided with an unusual background—a freely treated seascape—everything in the new picture was perfectly clear and incontrovertible.

The charm of the portrait lies, in the first place, in the subject itself, the pert naturalness of the girl. Her dark-brown eyes and dark eyebrows together with her pale complexion create a perfect harmony with her blond to reddish hair and reddish-brownish lozenge-patterned gold-trimmed dress with its quite low-cut squarish neck opening. Over the back of her hair she wears a snood, and her long locks tumble down over her ears. On her shoulders are pinned ribbon bows, tan on the left, dark greenish blue on the right, and they spill across the billowing white fillets of her blouse. As a final touch she wears a loose-hanging necklace of rhomboid-shaped black stones alternating with double strands of pearls. All told, women's fashions had not changed much since the ink sketches the artist had done on his first visit to Venice eleven years before.

THE MADONNA BEFORE ARCHED WALLS

Panel, $18^7/_8 \times 14^1/_8''$

Capuchin Monastery, Bagnacavallo, near Ravenna

Considering how little one might have expected it, recent years have been far from poor in new discoveries of works by Dürer. But the great and happy surprise was the finding of this Madonna and Child in a little-frequented church in Italy. The picture dates from the artist's second Italian sojourn, and this is the first time it is discussed in a non-Italian publication. All in all, the painting is so convincingly typical and of such high quality that it is not surprising that Roberto Longhi, who first described it in an Italian journal, should have pronounced without hesitation the name of Dürer at the mere sight of a faded photograph shown him by his student Don Antonio Savioli.

Rejoicing at this new addition to the known works of Dürer was so much greater because of the unusually good state of preservation of the picture. A single bit of over-painting, the ridiculous "bathing trunks" of the Christ Child, could easily be cleaned off and so can be dismissed as irrelevant.

There are no difficulties in situating the picture among Dürer's works. That it was painted in Venice is obvious, and, as Longhi presumes, it must be earlier than *The Madonna of the Rose Garlands*, to which it is related as the bud to the flower, even taking into account the bad condition of the latter picture. The great charm of this wonderful painting lies in the tentative, as yet unstereotyped depiction of the Mother and Child and their gestures. This explains, among other things, the fact that the Child looks up toward His mother without, as one might expect, actually meeting her lowered gaze.

It is astonishing that Dürer, who painted, engraved, and drew so many Madonnas, should never once have repeated himself. In each of them there is something fresh and new, as here where the mother, supporting the infant with her right hand, takes his tiny left hand in hers, thereby creating a complex plastic union of the two figures.

Longhi has pointed out that the position of the Child very much resembles that in the *Madonna and Child* on the art market (fig. 7) discussed in our text. That picture dates from almost a decade earlier, and in the present work the feeling for plastic values is much more advanced, even if not yet as fully developed as it was soon to be.

THE MADONNA OF THE ROSE GARLANDS
(detail of the head of a donor)

Panel, 63³⁄₄ × 76⁹⁄₁₆"

National Gallery, Prague

The Madonna of the Rose Garlands (see fig. 16)—which might also be called "The Feast of the Confraternity of the Rosary"—is conceived as a hymn to Mary and the Christ Child who reward the highest dignitaries of Church and State with garlands of roses.

The youthful Mother of God, gowned in heavenly lapis lazuli and with two tiny angels holding a crown above her head, sits enthroned before a purple baldachin. The Child in her lap is in the act of placing a garland on the head of the kneeling Pope, Julius II. Balancing the Pope, on the right kneels Emperor Maximilian I on whom Mary herself bestows a garland. Between the two worshiping potentates sits an angel playing a lute, a figure clearly derived from Giovanni Bellini. To the right and the left of the principal personages and behind them are grouped other worshipers and the donors of the altarpiece, over whom tiny angels bearing garlands swarm like bees. Only St. Dominic, who instituted this special cult, rises above the invisible but implicit horizontal line which articulates the picture into two halves. He himself crowns Cardinal Grimani, the Patriarch of Venice. At the far right to the rear are the smaller figures of Dürer himself and a companion, and behind them a mountainous landscape.

Unfortunately it must be admitted that the picture is in a virtually ruined state. Only the beautiful sections with trees in the upper left have been spared. As early as an inventory of 1718 it was listed as entirely ruined. So true is this, that a good photograph brings out more than can be seen with the naked eye. We can only hope that some day a first-class restorer may be able to clean off the repainting and reveal whatever remains of the true quality of the picture.

Under the circumstances, it is lucky that a great many preparatory brush drawings have survived, mostly on Venetian blue paper with white highlights, among them the head and mantle of the Pope, the St. Dominic, the figures identified as Van Heygh—the kneeling chief donor (whom we see in this color detail)—and the architect Hieronymus of Augsburg (who may have built the hall of the German merchants), plus heads and hands of angels.

To protect the picture, Emperor Rudolph II ordered it to be removed from Venice around 1600, and it was carried over the Alps to Prague on the shoulders of four strong men. Later, to keep it from the Swedish in the course of the war, it was taken elsewhere for safekeeping—and thereby ruined. When it was finally returned to Prague, it was sold at auction in 1782 for the ridiculous sum of one florin, eighteen kreuzers.

Painted 1507

ADAM AND EVE

Panels, 82¹/₄×31⁷/₈" and 82¹/₄×32⁵/₈"

The Prado, Madrid

When in 1507 Dürer set about to do large-scale paintings of our first ancestors, some years had elapsed since he had dealt with the same subject in a copperplate engraving (fig. 12) which was the end product of innumerable studies in classical proportions. What interested him was not showing how the first humans may really have looked—that remained for Rembrandt—but rather presenting them as God's creatures. This meant that they must be paragons of beauty, and for Dürer the secret of divinity lay in perfection of proportions.

Dürer would not have been the great artist he was if in these paintings he had merely repeated what he had done before. In the intervening years his studies had been pushed much further, and if in 1504 he still believed in the unique and quintessential beautiful human figure—"whether man or woman"—in the meantime he had come to understand that there was not a single canon of beauty but, instead, a multitude of possible proportions which must be welded into their own types of stylistic unity. Drawings dated 1506 have survived with nudes constructed according to this theory (W 423–28). Now Dürer's ideal figure is more slender, and this he realized in these two nudes.

Eve is still presented frontally, but the simple reposeful stance in the engraving, with weight distributed unequally between the fixed and the free leg, is rejected here in favor of a lighter grace, almost a balletic movement with the left foot directly behind the right. In the engraving her head was in profile, her searching gaze fixed on the apple. Here, as a consequence of Dürer's new feeling for the nude, the position is more frontal and Eve's expression softened into one of vague and uncertain expectation.

The sun-bronzed Adam's pose likewise is less secure, and his head is in three-quarter profile to the right. In contrast to the power characterizing Adam in the engraving, what Dürer seems to stress here is the inner torment of the unredeemed First Father. The fingers of his right hand are extended like those of a man who tests the water before entering it, and the branch which taught him shame is dangled almost playfully. In this respect, too, Eve is more than a match for him: she reaches for the apple without so much as looking at it and with elegant nonchalance rests her weight on a bough of the fatal tree.

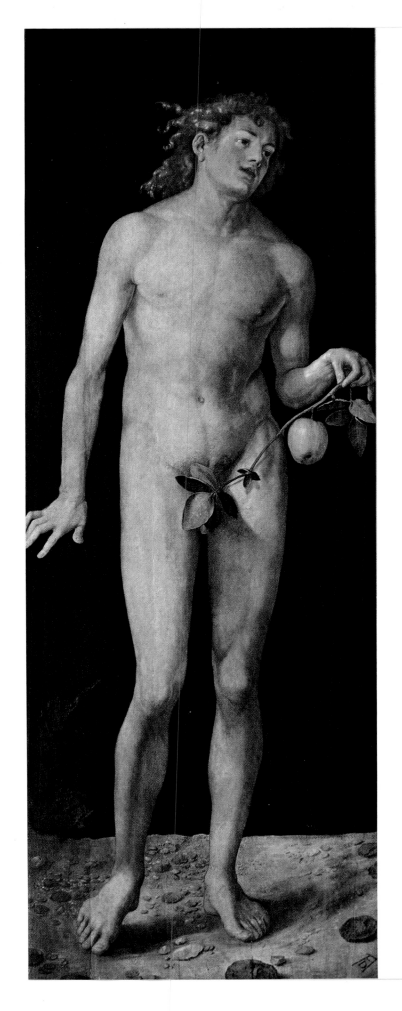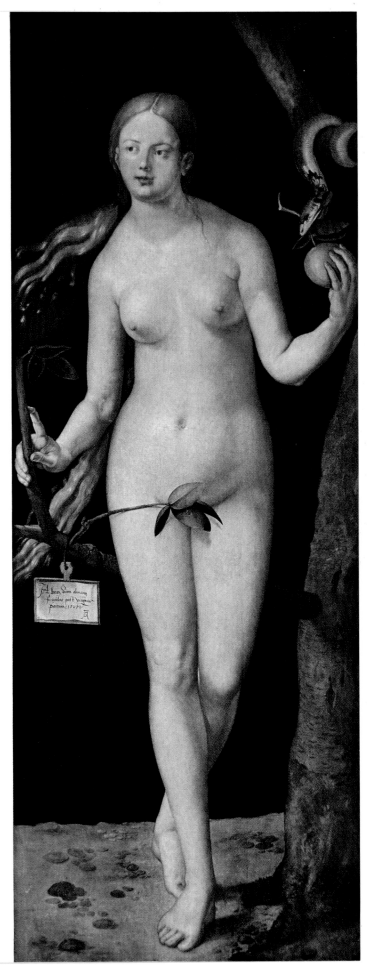

Painted 1511

THE ALL SAINTS ALTARPIECE
(The Adoration of the Trinity, detail)

Panel, 56³/₄ × 51⁵/₈"

Kunsthistorisches Museum, Vienna

Since the *Heller Altarpiece* was burned and *The Madonna of the Rose Garlands* allowed to go to ruin, the *All Saints Altarpiece* (see fig. 22) takes on special importance as an example of a painting with numerous figures which express a subject of great seriousness. Thausing called it "the last German act of homage before the Reformation to an as yet intact Roman Catholic system."

In the Vienna museum it glows like a jewel and holds its own among the great paintings of all countries, a beautifully interpreted hymn to a humanity capable of approaching divinity. Unforgettable is the extraordinary hiatus in the composition: the Trinity soaring aloft amid a choir of angels and saints, the world of man below, it too peopled by a multitude of the blessed.

The subject is drawn from a vision of St. Augustine's in which he beheld the *civitas dei* as it would be after the Last Judgment when the earthly community of man becomes reunited with the realm of Heaven. The Last Judgment itself is carved on the frame of the picture, now in Nuremberg.

Although the picture is not especially large, it radiates immensely, its effect heightened by the gold touches added to its lavish coloring from which all dark shadows have been banished. There are strokes of genius in the picture: the enlargement of the scale of the figures in the lower half; the introduction of a back view of the Pope in gold-brocaded cape and, at his side, a cardinal in vermilion who beckons to the humbly gray-clad donor Matthias Landauer as if to invite him to partake of the feast of the saints. The concept is further dramatized in the symmetrical group where the Emperor in all his majesty, mantled in yellow silk with sumptuous trimming of mink and gowned in carmine shot with white, points out the celestial spectacle to his Co-Emperor in crimson with gray fur (this in itself is something unheard of on earth, and to match it there is a second Pope on the left). The remaining space is crammed with the representatives of the Frankish estates, among whom is a knight in gold armor (a portrait of the donor's son-in-law), a peasant with a flail whom another figure instructs in the proper comportment in such august company, and a bevy of charming women.

In his almost contemporary *Disputa*, Raphael aimed at a similar conception. But while the Italian never truly succeeded in rising above the earthly sphere, the German was able to give form to a truly celestial vision. Dürer carried further the tradition the Van Eyck brothers began with *The Adoration of the Lamb* in Ghent, and it is no more than just that he should portray himself proudly as a tiny figure in the landscape below, above which soar like living men the spirits taken up into Heaven.

Painted 1512

MADONNA AND CHILD WITH A PEAR

Panel, 19 $\frac{1}{4} \times 14\frac{5}{8}$″

Kunsthistorisches Museum, Vienna

In Dürer's various stages of development, his representations of the Virgin range from the simplest of maidens to the Queen of Heaven with scepter and crown. As an example of the more homely poetic type there is the engraving of the nursing *Madonna by the Fence* of 1503 (B 34), and this was preceded some years earlier by the highly formalistic *Madonna with the Monkey* (B 42) which derives from principles Dürer acquired in Italy.

After his second Italian sojourn, several years went by before his expression regained its former vitality, and there is perhaps no more effective illustration for that than this Madonna with the Child who clutches half of a pear.

The painting hovers at the borderline where concern with form threatens to turn into mannerism, and so is quite unlike the exquisitely naïve Bagnacavallo Madonna (page 101). In the present painting the contrasts are more marked than in the brush drawing (W 388) done in Venice and used as a study for *The Madonna of the Rose Garlands*, and that is why we cannot entertain seriously the proposal that it was used again for this work. The completely naked Child (the little veil over the loins is a ridiculous later addition which could easily be removed) is as jerkily animated as a marionette. His hair is downy, pale blond, and curly, His nose turned up, two tiny teeth can be made out between His bright-red parted lips, and He gazes alertly out of clear dark eyes while His mother looks down at Him. He lies stretched out on a piece of fabric shading from white to light blue held by the mother's left hand, of which no more than two fingers can be seen. For compositional purposes, part of the cloth on the left was made much lighter and stands out against the dark background.

The Child is held like an offering, and one can read in the mother's face her concern that no ill befall Him. She herself is utterly lovely though somewhat affected, with her high-arched eyebrows and cherry-red mouth. Her veil is a little disarrayed and tumbles down over her forehead and the circlet binding her flowing hair which on the left is somewhat fuller than on the right, where corkscrew curls twist perpendicularly downward to make a necessary formal contrast. A formal function is likewise fulfilled by the square neck opening of her bright-blue dress.

WING OF A BLUE ROLLER

Watercolor and gouache on vellum, $7^3/_4 \times 7^7/_8''$

Albertina, Vienna

One of the finest things in the *Nemesis* engraving is the plumage on the right wing of the nude woman who soars above the earth poised on a sphere. The engraving was done around 1502, so it appears likely that Dürer had already become interested in plumage and done studies of it. The studies in the Escorial (W I, plate XXIII), one of which is dated 1500, are of obviously fine quality, but Winkler hesitated to make a positive attribution to Dürer, and this was the case also with the studies of birds of paradise in London and Erlangen (W II, plates XII, XIII). Further research is needed to decide if they are really by Dürer and, if so, if they date from his early period.

Dürer's interest in feathers and all sorts of sensuously attractive objects comes out in the letters he wrote from Venice to his friend Willibald Pirckheimer, in which he often complained that he could not get hold of certain types of feathers he wanted very much to see, especially green ones and those from cranes.

One of the most painstakingly worked-out studies of this sort is this *Wing of a Blue Roller* (W 614), which was done at almost the same time as the *Blue Roller* (W 615), likewise in the Albertina. With unexampled accuracy and great understanding, each and every feather is characterized in color—brilliant blue alternating with emerald green—and in every small sameness and difference, with the result that its particular function in flight is made perfectly clear. One sees how the shorter feathers overlap and protect the longer, how as they approach the bone and muscles they become much more numerous and downy, while closer to the breast broader feathers hang down in tufts.

Dürer painted this study on vellum, which is always an indication of his special concern, and he carefully dated it 1512 and signed it.

PORTRAIT OF A YOUNG MAN

Panel, $16^3/_4 \times 13^5/_8$"

Fine Arts Museum, Budapest

The German paintings in the Budapest museum are especially numerous and of unusually high quality. Upon entering the room of the earlier German masters, one's attention is caught by a portrait of a young man that one knows could only be by Dürer. It has been proposed that the sitter was Dürer's brother Endres, but comparison with the portrait drawing of 1514 (W 558) in no way bears this out. Endres had a squarish face, a large nose (though not as prominent as Albrecht's), and a short upper lip. The young man portrayed here is much more the man-about-town with his frank friendly eyes, high-arched eyebrows, straight nose, and quite unusual asymmetrical mouth with its vaguely humorous smile. To claim a passage of years between the drawing and the painting does not explain the differences in physiognomy, since both portraits must have been done at roughly the same period.

The blond young man has a healthy complexion inclining to ruddiness. His already high forehead is accentuated by a loosely crocheted black wool skullcap with a narrow black-and-white headband which is worn so high as to let us see just the first strands of his flaxen hair. His shaggy black fur collar stands out sharply against the deep vermilion background.

The head is modeled with exquisite finesse and could serve as an illustration for the passage in the draft for an appendix on aesthetics in the third book of Dürer's *Human Proportions*, where he speaks about how remarkably round the head is: "And so the forehead, cheeks, nose, eyes, mouth, and chin, with all their indentations and convexities, should be brought out with particular care." Nothing sums up better the difference between the master and even his best pupils, for it is precisely this they lack. It is a worthwhile experience to examine the original of this portrait through a hand lens. Only thus can one really appreciate Dürer's technique, how every brush stroke is almost like the stroke of a pen and always perfect, never corrected, and how, when observed from a certain distance, all the separate strokes coalesce to create an extraordinary, truly fascinating, and entirely painterly impression.

Painted 1516

MICHAEL WOLGEMUT

Panel, 11⁷/₁₆ × 10⁵/₈"

Germanisches Nationalmuseum, Nuremberg

Generally Dürer preferred a vertical rectangular format for his portraits, but for this one of his teacher Wolgemut he chose an almost perfect square, and we are struck by how the compression of space brings out the wasted visage of the old man. Indeed, it is impossible to imagine it otherwise.

Michael Wolgemut was not only a draftsman and painter but also the head of a workshop which turned out many large altarpieces. Dürer learned more than the craft of painting there. He could also observe, step by step, how such important books as the *Schatzbehalter* and Schedel's *Weltchronik* were produced, and he perhaps helped on them. Wolgemut was a man who worked hard and much, an outstanding, highly responsible craftsman in the best tradition of the Late Gothic, an age of collective enterprise, and he was also a painter of significance. When Dürer portrayed him in 1516, he was eighty-two years old and still had three years of life ahead of him. We know today that in his youth Wolgemut was active in Munich and had ambitions to marry the daughter of Gabriel Mälesskircher, his master there, who would have left a considerable fortune to the girl.

The man is wasted almost to the bone, his eyes are sunk in shadowy hollows, his upper lip recedes over his toothless mouth. The chin is still well defined, but the skin hangs in great folds over the neck. The nose is somewhat hooked but slender and elegant, the ear partly hidden by his stylish, close-fitting, turban-like silk cap from under which emerge a few stray hairs not at all grayed. Over his white shirt and black jacket he wears a fox-fur shawl. The thoughtfulness, intelligence, and undemonstrativeness of this unassuming human being could not be better expressed.

It was after the death of his teacher that Dürer added the lengthy circumstantial inscription.

Painted 1516

HEAD OF AN APOSTLE (Philip)

Tempera on canvas, 17³/₄ × 15"
Uffizi Gallery, Florence

Unlike Baldung and Cranach who did complete series of the Apostles in woodcuts, even as late as his middle period Dürer had made no more than a start on such a project with his copperplate engravings of Paul and Thomas done in 1514. Not until 1523 did he add to the series Bartholomew, Simon, and Philip (fig. 41, but note that the date on the engraving was altered to 1526). The preparatory drawings he did for these engravings served later for his last and greatest achievement, the paintings of the four Apostles (pages 139 and 141).

In the meantime, in 1516, he painted the imposing *Philip* and *James Major* now in the Uffizi which, although done in tempera on canvas, are excellently preserved.

The two paintings are much alike. Both Apostles are emotionally agitated, God-possessed. Philip is presented closer to the viewer, and one gets the impression that he has suddenly whipped his head around, his brow wrinkled, his eyes heavy with sorrow, his mouth dropped open. It is as if he were compelled to gaze upon something which stirred his indignation.

The *James* is like an intensification of the *Philip*, as if only here was the master able truly to bring out his conception, or at least to express it with full clarity. James is older, set deeper into the background, his bare skull bulging enormously at the forehead, his eyes more shadowed, more sorrowful, his opened mouth more expressive of suffering, his rocklike face sunk in the snowy glacier of his beard.

In each of these, Dürer succeeded in expressing the inexpressible, that which possesses a man to become a Man of God. The types he was able to create are the visual personifications of spiritual attributes. The immense beards, especially James's, assume a formal supporting function. White as foaming spray, as Winkler put it, they go beyond what is possible to become something surrealist, like the St. Anthony in Grünewald's Isenheim altarpiece. Their beards are metamorphosed into independent, virtually abstract forms which, like secondary melodies in music, accompany the principal theme.

SANCTE.
PRONOBIS

PHILIPPE ORATE
1516 AD

Painted 1518

THE VIRGIN IN PRAYER

Panel, 20⁷/₈ × 16⁷/₈"

State Museums, Berlin-Dahlem

This picture is virtually an illustration of Dürer's theory: "And as they [the Ancients] depicted Venus as the most beautiful of women, so too—but chastely—do we aspire to portray the most pure Virgin Mary, God's mother." It is, in fact, the perfect illustration of that theory. Here Dürer sets down exactly what he means when he speaks of the most beautiful of maidens. "Beautiful" for him does not have its modern connotations but is something more like "full of grace." Mary is a mature young woman with a healthy, tanned complexion, frank plain features, and the porcelain-like brown eyes mirroring her candid soul which are characteristic of Dürer's late works. The hands are not those of a fine lady but rather almost peasant-like, and they are especially carefully modeled, almost more than the face itself.

She wears an ice-green headkerchief over which she has drawn her blue mantle in such a way that we see almost more of its orange lining which, in the shadows, deepens into red. Her sleeves, rose-colored highlighted with white, emerge through slits in her bright cobalt-blue mantle. Here one sees how carefully Dürer avoided shadowing. Even where there must be shadow, he remained within the spectrum of the local color. Nor is any landscape background possible here where what is aimed at is an ideal image. Instead he chose a strongly colored neutral background which a vertical yellow double stripe divides into a bright reddish-brown area on the left and, on the right, a broad plane which blends from yellowish olive-green to grass-green in the shadows.

The painting was probably originally designed as the right-hand panel of a diptych with Christ on the left.

The pleats in the headkerchief, the mantle drawn loosely about the figure, the tight shirring of the wristbands, all of which are motifs typical of the later engravings, work together to intensify the impression of monumentality.

EMPEROR MAXIMILIAN I

Tempera on canvas, 32⁵/₈ × 25⁵/₈"
Germanisches Nationalmuseum, Nuremberg

For Emperor Maximilian, who was himself something of a writer, the company of learned men and artists was an indispensable part of life, and he devoted a considerable share of his very limited leisure to the arts. We owe to Melanchthon a charming description of him in 1499 which goes back to information from Pirckheimer: once, while sailing across Lake Constance, Maximilian passed the time dictating the text of the *Weisskunig* in Latin and urged his companion to tell him frankly if he was satisfied with his *militaris latinitas*, his "soldiers' Latin." Quite early he entered into relations with artists who were mostly from Augsburg, above all with Hans Burgkmair, of whom Dürer painted a portrait, now lost, and also did a drawing (W 569, in Berlin). Probably it was through Burgkmair that the Emperor came to know about Dürer, to whom he was to award such major commissions as the designs for the prayer book, the *Triumphal Arch*, and the *Triumphal Procession*.

On June 8, 1518, the Emperor sat for the portrait drawing (W 567) now in the Albertina which bears this inscription: "This is Emperor Maximilian whom I, Albrecht Dürer, portrayed in Augsburg in his little room high up in the castle in the year 1518 on the Monday after St. John's day."

That drawing provided the basis for the Vienna and Nuremberg painted portraits of the Emperor, who died on January 12, 1519, as well as for the beautiful gold-plate woodcut portrait of which only four copies remain (complete in Bamberg and Gotha, lacking the inscription in Gotha and London), though it was widely diffused in later cuts.

In his Netherlands journal Dürer mentions a portrait of Maximilian which he wished to offer as a gift to the Emperor's vice-regent in Brussels, Archduchess Margaret of Austria, "but since she was so displeased with it, I took it back." We do not know which of the two portraits this was or if there was a third, nor the grounds for her disapproval, though she probably did not find it a good likeness—in which we are convinced she was wrong.

The first portrait done was the Nuremberg version, for which a study for the hands with the pomegranate exists (W 635), and it was executed more rapidly since here Dürer used tempera on canvas. While it may lack the polished, definitive quality of the Vienna version, it is more personal, more human. Despite its deplorable state and the fact that its forms, which are relatively less decisive, have sunk into the canvas, it still conveys some idea of how beautiful once was the tiger-lily-red shading down to incarnadine of the wide mantle against the cobalt-blue background (which has grown rather murky), and how beautifully executed were the fine strands of graying hair emerging from under the broad black hat.

Painted 1519

MADONNA AND CHILD WITH ST. ANNE

Transferred from panel to canvas, $23^5/_8 \times 19^5/_8$"

The Metropolitan Museum of Art, New York (Bequest of Benjamin Altman)

Here is one of Dürer's supreme masterworks, and it has come down to us in immaculate condition. Until 1852 it was in the Schleissheim gallery but then, incredible as it seems, because its authenticity was questioned it was sold at auction into a Russian private collection in Odessa and finally came to New York in the Altman collection.

Like a youngster almost, maidenly, hands joined in prayer, Mary worships her Child, of whom scarcely more than the tiny dreaming head is visible. The Child lies on the right arm of St. Anne who is swathed, in Nuremberg fashion, in a full-hooded garment. Her left arm caresses the shoulder of her blessed daughter.

The Child sleeps. Perhaps never again did anyone depict so beautifully in paint the sleep of a child watched over by mother and grandmother.

The ice-green of St. Anne's hood, the greenish white of her neckcloth, Mary's garment shimmering between white and whitish red and set off by deep blue, the vermilion fabric on which the Child is laid, all these would reveal their full beauty were it not that, in the Romantic period apparently, a varnish was overlaid which robbed something from the original freshness of the colors and the clarity and decisiveness of the forms. A cautious cleaning would probably do wonders here.

A large brush drawing in the Albertina (W 574) is correctly identified as a study for the St. Anne but less convincingly as a portrait of Dürer's wife. The chief traits of St. Anne in the painting—the flattened nose and wide mouth—are lacking in the drawing, and of course Agnes Dürer did not have the porcelain doll's eyes typical of Dürer's later works, in which he aimed at deliberate idealization of holy figures.

JAKOB FUGGER

Tempera on canvas, 26³/₄ × 20¹/₂″

Alte Pinakothek, Munich (formerly Staatliche Gemäldegalerie, Augsburg)

Emperors, kings, princes, and great gentlemen sent emissaries to him. The Pope greeted him as his beloved son and embraced him. He laid the economic foundations for the Hapsburgs' European policy and financed the election of Charles V as emperor. But Luther said someone ought to ram a bridle into his mouth, and Ulrich von Hutten dubbed him Prince of Courtesans and Robber Baron.

The viewer exclaims: Yes, that is how he must have looked, that is how he was! His eyes are crafty as those of a lynx promoted to be king of the beasts, but in his face one can read also the self-discipline and passion for work without which he could never have won such power nor held it. For his portrait Jakob Fugger deliberately put on the simplest of garments, but by emphasizing the very wide crisscrossed collar of the fur-lined mantle the painter sought to endow the figure with a breadth and monumentality which recall the portraits by Titian. The gold-embroidered cap is itself a small reminder of the sitter's wealth.

Like most paintings in tempera on canvas, this picture has deteriorated somewhat, but it is superior in form and in its revelation of Fugger's character to the equally poorly preserved drawing in Berlin (W 571). Since we know that there was once another portrait drawing of him in the possession of Sandrart together with one of Fugger's wife Sybille, born Arzt, and since the pose is more sidewise than in the Berlin drawing, it is far from certain that the latter was the preparatory study for this painting. The drawing does not elevate the sitter above the common run of men into someone special and unique as does the painting. The portrait can be dated 1520 on the basis of a copy which bears that date.

Painted 1521

ST. JEROME

Panel, 23⁵/₈ × 18⁷/₈"

National Museum, Lisbon

In a cramped room sits the Saint old as time, wrapped in his crimson cardinal's robe, head propped on right hand, an open book before him. Despondently he stares out of the picture at us and points with his index finger at a death's-head, the symbol of the fleetingness of life. The ledge he sits behind is there, as so often in Dürer's pictures, to create an illusion of depth, as are also many other details: the small lectern with books piled underneath it, the foreshortened open volume, the skull lying on its side, the window sill and frame with the crucifix.

Through these means Dürer exploited the half-figure treatment common in the Netherlands but made it so much his own that this picture itself came in turn to be widely imitated.

The thousands of gleaming silver rivulets of the beard and the ingrained wrinkles of the face contrast with the sleekly smooth mass of the bluish-green headpiece. Stiff in every joint, the aged man moves painfully. Only his eyes, but not his head, swivel around to look at us.

The picture was painted in 1521, in the Netherlands, as a gift to the Portuguese agent Rodrigo d'Almada with whom Dürer had become great friends in Antwerp and whom he portrayed in a drawing (W 813). For his part, the envoy often gladdened the life of the artist with gifts of exotic preserves, peaches, quince slices, strong wines, oysters, and the like from his southern homeland. "I worked hard at a St. Jerome in oil and gave it as a gift to Rodrigo of Portugal, who gave Susanna (the maid) a ducat as a gratuity" is what he says about it in his journal. This explains how the picture came to be the great glory of the Lisbon museum.

The painting was especially carefully prepared by white-highlighted brush drawings on dark-violet paper, most of which are in the Albertina: the left forearm with the pointing finger (W 790), the lectern with the books (W 791), and the death's-head (W 792; Dürer made a special point of noting that he had to lay out two "white pennies" for the skull). The preliminary studies for the Saint himself include one sketch from life, now lost, and two master drawings: the famous portrait in the Albertina of a ninety-three-year-old man (W 788) and the less well-known gnome's face in Berlin (W 789) which rather more resembles the painting since the eyes are opened wide as here. The particularly painstaking work he put in on the Albertina drawing reminds us of his own words: "Every single part must be worked out with the utmost observation and care in the tiniest details as much as in the largest. For this reason I urge you to follow this counsel and not to play fast and loose with what you find in nature."

Painted 1521

BERNHARD VON RESTEN

Panel, 17⁷/₈ × 12³/₈"

Staatliche Gemäldegalerie, Dresden

Bernhard von Resten is mentioned twice in Dürer's Netherlands journal. Under the date of December 10, 1520, we learn that Dürer portrayed him in Antwerp, under that of March 16, 1521, that he "counterfeited" him in oil colors—"and he gave me eight florins for it and to my wife a crown and to Susanna (the maid) a florin." There can be no doubt that this refers to the present painting. Who Bernhard von Resten was we do not know, but he must have been wealthy. Certainly, not all of Dürer's patrons behaved so gallantly. The earlier notion that the sitter was the painter Bernhard (Barent) van Orley has been pretty much rejected. The portrait drawing (W 810) Dürer did of his younger colleague in Brussels shows a quite different physiognomy, the mouth in particular being quite dissimilar.

The portrait of the young man in furs and dark hat against a red background is one of Dürer's finest and best preserved. It is difficult to understand how a scholar like Eduard Flechsig, who, especially on the basis of this portrait, clarified so many questions, could have been led to say, because of the considerable breadth of the face resulting from the unusually prominent cheekbones, that the man's features are ugly. For us, the young man with candid gaze and firm-set mouth who holds in his hand some sort of paper—was he a merchant, an agent, or something we cannot guess?—is a representative of a happier age, which shook off the Middle Ages and encouraged mankind to an awareness of its own high worth.

Painted 1521

JOBST PLANCKFELT

Panel, $19^5/_8 \times 14^1/_8$"
The Prado, Madrid

There is much controversy about the date of this portrait and the identity of the sitter. The Prado catalogue gives the date as 1524, but some observers are inclined to read the last digit, which is rather difficult to make out, as 1. The panel seems to be of oak rather than the linden wood Dürer generally used in Nuremberg.

These two factors support Eduard Flechsig's contention that this is the portrait referred to in the Netherlands journal of mid-May 1521: "Item, Jobst, my host, neatly and carefully counterfeited in oil colors."

Dürer also did a drawing of Planckfelt (W 747), and at first glance the connection between that small sheet and the painted portrait is not entirely clear. However, if we take into account that, in the one case, we have a quickly sketched brush drawing showing the innkeeper as he went about his daily business and, in the other, a painting of some importance for which the sitter got himself up, so to speak, in gala attire, we find that the two have so much in common that Flechsig's proposal seems amply justified. There was between Dürer and his host a close relationship, a genuine friendship. They exchanged gifts, among which was the portrait, and Dürer took his meals with him alone, without his wife. This suggests a personality rather above the average, which must have appealed to the artist. As for the identification of the subject as Hans Imhoff the Elder, which goes back to Thausing, it was firmly refuted by Flechsig, and Winkler's suggestion of Pirckheimer has likewise failed to stand up.

This point clarified, nothing prevents recognizing the close affinity between this portrait and that of Lorenz Sterck in the Isabella Stewart Gardner Museum of Boston. The paintings are similar not only in treatment of externals (fur, mantle, hat, position of the hands) but even more in the thoroughgoing painterly conception which was typical of Dürer's style during his sojourn in the Netherlands.

992.

Painted 1526

MADONNA AND CHILD

Panel, 16⁷/₈ × 12⁵/₈"

Uffizi Gallery, Florence

Dürer did many more engraved than painted Madonnas. The painting in Dresden of the Virgin in veneration before the Child (page 71) is a prelude to all the others. One of the earliest, which is currently on the art market and was described in *Paragone* in 1961, is poorly preserved. It was discovered only a few years ago, and its finding was preceded by a few years by that of another Madonna, the so-called Haller Madonna in Washington, D.C. In the latter, a poorly formed infant stands stretching rather clumsily and is held by a Madonna very much in the Italian manner, and this is quite unlike the intimate charm of the small panel in Vienna from 1503. In Venice in 1506 Dürer did both the *Madonna with the Siskin*, now in Berlin and in bad condition, and the very beautiful, still scarcely known *Madonna before Arched Walls* in Bagnacavallo (page 101) which represents the style of his Venetian period in purest form. As might be expected since Joseph also figures in it, the small panel from 1509 in Rotterdam has a heartier feeling about it, while the Vienna Madonna of 1512 (page 109) is more formalistic and the one in Munich from 1518 stresses the constructivistic aspects.

Two years before his death, Dürer achieved the work we have here in which all of his various preoccupations were finally synthesized. In it, consummate formal sense is allied with complete naturalness, and superb craftsmanship is placed at the service of simple sentiment. The maidenly mother with lowered eyelids and ripe cherry-mouth, dressed in delicate rose, faces directly forward and holds an apple in her left hand. The Child in a dress of gray, shot with green, stares alertly at the fruit while His mother supports Him on her right arm, which we cannot see.

132

Painted 1526

HIERONYMUS HOLZSCHUHER

Panel, 18⁷/₈ × 14¹/₈″

State Museums, Berlin-Dahlem

Hieronymus Holzschuher was a member of the Nuremberg town council, a "Septemvir" charged with certain high functions, an early partisan of Luther and a friend of Dürer who brought him a large horn as a souvenir of the Netherlands. He was also linked by friendship and religious conviction with Jakob Muffel, whom Dürer portrayed with equal mastery in the same year of 1526 (page 137). In those two busts, of a greater pictorial solidity than those done in the Netherlands, Dürer reached the highest point possible to him in portraiture. They are what, in Venice twenty years before, he dreamed of achieving: works in "high relief," that is, of plastic, physical solidity such as to deceive the eye. Near them in the Berlin gallery hangs a portrait by Hans von Kulmbach. Comparison reveals the enormous gap between genius and routine talent.

The squarish cuboid head sits neckless on shoulders draped in bristly fox fur against a background shading from pale vitriol to blue. The complexion is clear compared with the sanguine, almost coppery complexion of the Muffel portrait. The water-blue eyes under the vertically furrowed brow turn to look sharply and critically out of the picture. What is perhaps rendered with the most minute exactitude is the nose, sloping down straight, somewhat pointed, all its details finely delineated. The mouth is proud and stubborn, the underlip full and rather protruding. Cheeks and forehead are treated with exceptionally plastic modeling and are brimming with a vitality which gives the lie to the sitter's gray-white hair, though even that retains a strand or two of youthful blond as it tumbles down hiding the ears with a few locks falling across the forehead. The small drooping moustache ends in almost wholly white crinkly chin whiskers. All this is sharply contrasted formally with the narrow white edge of shirt which forms the horizontal base for the inverted triangle of the collar opening. The eyes and eyebrows suggest a stormy temperament, but the firmly set mouth reveals self-mastery. Dürer seems to have made his point: the man himself is all of a piece and stolid as a bull—but woe to him who dares to wave a red flag. With such a personality, it is not surprising that many have found Holzschuher a more typical German than the more contemplative Jakob Muffel. The mature art of a great master is, as in this case, by no means affected by the character of the man he portrays. The picture has won its just fame because of the consummate mastery of its creator, not because Hieronymus Holzschuher, for all his personal magnetism, was a model of mankind, though no one questions his qualities.

Painted 1526

JAKOB MUFFEL

Transferred from panel to canvas, $18^7/_8 \times 14^1/_8''$

State Museums, Berlin-Dahlem

Once again in this portrait the sitter is posed turned toward the left as was Dürer's custom in his late works. While this may tend to a certain monotony, perhaps it was done for the same reason as induced the artist for a long time to light his engravings from the left.

Although Jakob Muffel occupied the same position in the Nuremberg council as Hieronymus Holzschuher, he was a man of quite different stamp. He too took his duties seriously, and one senses that the man, with all his deeply human traits, shouldered heavy responsibilities and was no less worthy than Holzschuher of the high office he was called on to exercise in troubled times of social and religious rebellion and fanaticism. And yet one suspects that he discharged his functions with rather more sensitivity than his colleague.

Dominating intelligence can be read in his broad vaulted forehead whose roundness is accentuated by the gold braid encircling his skullcap, which itself touches the upper edge of the picture, and his keen-sensed nose suggests alertness to detail. The troubled dark eyes and the firm-set, thin-lipped, almost grieving mouth belong to a man of few words and not inclined to rash decisions but who, when decisions had to be made, knew how to give apt counsel.

The white shirt, which, in contrast to the Holzschuher portrait, is loose and flowing, sets off the beauty of the yellowish-brown sable shawl which hangs unclasped across Muffel's shoulders. The luminous night-blue of the background could not have been better chosen to contrast with the rather coppery complexion of the sitter.

Painted 1526

THE FOUR APOSTLES

Panels, 84⁷/₈ × 29⁷/₈″ and 84¹/₂ × 29⁷/₈″
Alte Pinakothek, Munich

These two large panels were Dürer's gift to the city of Nuremberg. For a hundred years they hung in the council chamber of the town hall where the highest, non-elective officials held their deliberations. But then in 1627 the Elector Maximilian I of Bavaria decided that the pictures would not go at all badly in his collection. He put such strong pressure on Nuremberg that the council's resistance was broken. They had no choice except to make the best of a bad bargain and send the pictures to Munich—after themselves having to foot the bill for board and lodging for the Elector's emissaries! However, the good citizens of Nuremberg still had one hope: an integral part of the two pictures consisted of panels inscribed with lengthy texts, and those texts contained an explicit "warning to all secular princes" to respect God's word—that is, God's word as the Reformation saw it—and so it was thought that these could not fail to arouse the indignation of the Munich Jesuits, who would see to it that the pictures were returned where they belonged. But the Elector simply kept the pictures and sent back the inscribed panels, and it was not until 1922 that pictures and texts were reassembled. The controversial panels were beautifully lettered by the writing master Neudörfer with texts chosen from the Apocalypse, various Epistles, and the Gospel according to Mark. The texts were selected in line with Luther's doctrine, and have to do with the unperverted word of God, prophesying that the false teachings will be separated off from the true. They declare how the real spirit of God can be recognized and inveigh against the evil doings of those who dispossess widows of their houses and who love the pleasures of the senses more than they love God and yet go about disguised in the trappings of godliness.

These paintings were executed neither on commission nor for a church—and this in itself was something entirely new—but rather as an open affirmation of Dürer's own belief, to bear witness to his Evangelical faith, and to be a kind of spiritual testament. Dürer was on the one hand deeply impressed by Luther but, on the other, shocked by the mad confusion of the spirit stirred up by fanatics like Thomas Münzer and Hans Denk of Nuremberg and by the murderous consequences thereof. For those reasons he conceived his Apostles with the hope that they would serve as true models for human conduct. From the outset people tended to see in the four Apostles (though only John and Peter in fact deserve that title) allegorical embodiments of the Four Temperaments: John sanguine, Peter phlegmatic, Mark choleric, and Paul melancholy, but they do not really fit into those traditional types.

This is not to say that Dürer did not aim at differentiating them and contrasting them in their physiques and ages. How deeply he understood the broad bases of

(continued on page 140)

SELECTED BIBLIOGRAPHY

BARTSCH, ADAM. *Le Peintre Graveur.* Vol. VII, Vienna, 1808 (referred to in this book as: B).

BRUCK, ROBERT. *Das Skizzenbuch von Albrecht Dürer in der Kgl. Bibliothek zu Dresden.* 1905.

CARRITT, DAVID. "Dürer's 'St. Jerome in the Wilderness,'" *Burlington Magazine,* 1956, pp. 363 ff.

FLECHSIG, EDUARD. *Albrecht Dürer. Sein Leben und seine künstlerische Entwicklung.* 2 vols., Berlin, 1928, 1931.

FRAENGER, WILHELM. "Dürers Gedächtnissäule für den Bauernkrieg," *Albrecht Dürer. Die künstlerische Entwicklung eines grossen Meisters.* Berlin, 1954.

FRIEDLÄNDER, MAX J. *Albrecht Dürer.* Leipzig, 1921.

GIEHLOW, K. *Kaiser Maximilians I. Gebetbuch.* Vienna, 1907.

GLADECZEK, LEONHARD. *Albrecht Dürer und die Illustrationen zur Schedelchronik.* Baden-Baden, Strasbourg, 1965.

HEIDRICH, E. *Dürer und die Reformation.* Leipzig, 1909.

HOLZINGER, ERNST. "Von Körper und Raum bei Dürer und Grünewald," in Millard Meiss, ed., *Essays in Honor of Erwin Panofsky.* Vol. I, 1961.

KAUFFMANN, HANS. "Albrecht Dürers Dreikönigsaltar," *Wallraf-Richartz Jahrbuch.* 1938, pp. 166 ff.

KEHRER, HUGO. *Dürers Selbstbildnisse und die Dürerbildnisse.* Berlin, 1934.

KNAPPE, KARL-ADOLF. *Dürer. The Complete Engravings, Etchings, and Woodcuts.* New York, London, 1965.

KURTH, WILLI. *Dürers sämtliche Holzschnitte.* Munich, 1927 (*Albrecht Dürer: Complete Woodcuts.* New York, 1963).

LANGE, K., and F. FUHSE. *Dürers schriftlicher Nachlass.* Halle, 1903.

LEINZ, A., and V. DESSAUER. *Savonarola und Albrecht Dürer.* Munich, 1961.

LIPPMANN, FRIEDRICH. *Zeichnungen von Albrecht Dürer.* 7 vols., Berlin, 1883–1929.

LONGHI, ROBERTO. "Una Madonna del Dürer a Bagnacavallo," *Paragone,* July 1961.

MARTIN, KURT. *Albrecht Dürer: Die Vier Apostel.* Stuttgart, 1963.

MEDER, JOSEPH. *Dürer-Katalog. Ein Handbuch über Albrecht Dürers Stiche, Radierungen, Holzschnitte, deren Zustände, Ausgaben und Wasserzeichen.* Vienna, 1932.

MUSPER, H. TH. *Albrecht Dürer.* Stuttgart, 1953.

PANOFSKY, ERWIN. *Albrecht Dürer.* 2 vols., Princeton, 1948.

RUPPRICH, HANS. *Dürers schriftlicher Nachlass.* Vol. I, Berlin, 1956.

SCHILLING, EDMUND. "Dürers Täfelchen mit dem heiligen Hieronymus," *Zeitschrift für Kunstwissenschaft.* 1957, pp. 157 ff.

SCHULZ, FRITZ T. "Michael Wohlgemut," in Thieme-Becker, *Allgemeines Lexikon der bildenden Künstler.* Vol. 36, 1947.

STECK, MAX. *Albrecht Dürer: Schriften, Tagebücher, Briefe.* Stuttgart, 1961.

THAUSING, MORITZ. *Dürer.* 2 vols., Leipzig, 1884.

TIETZE, HANS, and ERICA TIETZE-CONRAT. *Kritisches Verzeichnis der Werke Albrecht Dürers.* Vol. I, Augsburg, 1928. Vol. II, nos. 1–2, Basel, Leipzig, 1937–38.

WAETZOLDT, WILHELM. *Dürer und seine Zeit.* Leipzig, 1935.

WINKLER, FRIEDRICH. *Die Zeichnungen Albrecht Dürers.* 4 vols., Berlin, 1936–39 (referred to in this book as: W).

———. *Albrecht Dürer. Leben und Werk.* Berlin, 1957.

———. "Verzeichnis der seit 1939 aufgefundenen Zeichnungen Dürers," *Festschrift für Dr. h.c. Eduard Trautscholdt.* Hamburg, 1965.

——— (ed.). *Dürer; des Meisters Gemälde, Kupferstiche und Holzschnitte* (Klassiker der Kunst, IV). 4th ed., Stuttgart, Leipzig, 1928.

WINZINGER, FRANZ. "Albrecht Dürers Münchener Selbstbildnis," *Zeitschrift für Kunstwissenschaft.* 1954.

WÖLFFLIN, HEINRICH. *Die Kunst Albrecht Dürers* (the most recent edition). Munich, 1964.

PHOTOGRAPHIC CREDITS